Richard Creagh-Osborne and I wrote our first book on the IYRU Rules in 1965, because they were not being interpreted in the same way in all countries. Many good races were ruined because of misunderstanding and lack of knowledge of the Rules. They are probably more complicated than in any other sport and any clarification can only benefit the racing yachtsman.

After Richard Creagh-Osborne's death in 1980 one of his good friends, Jonathan Bradbeer, undertook the editorial updating as the Rules evolved and were modified. For this I am very grateful.

Our most important task is to make the Rules so clear that we have a permanent picture of different racing situations firmly fixed in our heads.

It has been a struggle to make the Rules, as we know them today, but I believe that they actually cover all racing situations rather well. That is not to say they are all absolutely fair and it is difficult when one loses a place if someone else misjudges a mark, but yacht racing is and always has been a sport where gentlemanly behaviour is rated highly. To sail against others, in the same way we wish to be sailed against, is the greatest pleasure of racing—and leads to fewer problems with the Rules.

Paul Elvström

Paul Elvström in the 1984 Olympics with his daughter crewing.

OLYMPIC CHAMPION

1948	Firefly
1952	Finn
1956	Finn
1960	Finn

WORLD CHAMPION

1957	505
1958	505
1958	Finn
1959	Finn
1959	Snipe
1962	Flying Dutchman
1966	5.5
1966	Star
1967	Star
1969	Soling
1971	$\frac{1}{2}$ Ton
1974	Soling
1981	$\frac{1}{2}$ Ton

EUROPEAN CHAMPION

| 1983 | Tornado |
| 1984 | Tornado |

How to Get the Best Use Out of This Book

The book is divided into three sections.

1. The Yacht Racing Rules as published by the IYRU.

2. A simple explanation of the various situations that can arise under each rule, in some cases supported by bird's-eye line drawings.

3. A precis of many of the Interpretations of Appeals to the IYRU together in some instances with bird's-eye line drawings.

Following an incident, look up the appropriate Rule in the BLACK Section. This is a facsimile of the Rules. To avoid confusion, there is no comment in this section.

In the margin opposite the rule will be the cross reference page number printed in RED which refers you both to the Explanatory Section with RED thumb indexing and also to the relevant Interpretation Section with Red hatched thumb indexing.

The Explanatory Section is what it says – an explanation of the rule or rules involved, with line drawings to illustrate the points. To support these explanations are many of the Appeals to the IYRU. These form the Case Law for the Yacht Racing Rules and are an invaluable cross reference. It is recommended that both the serious competitor and also the student of the Rules, obtains a copy of these interpretations for the full text.

In the line drawings, the red or pink boat is either wrong, potentially wrong or in the worst position.

For quick reference, the various code flags used as signals in racing, and their meaning, are illustrated on the back cover.

I would like to thank the IYRU for their co-operation in producing this book.

Jonathan Bradbeer
January 1985

The 1985 Racing Rules—A summary of the alterations

Any system of Rules or Law evolves over a period of time. Those who administer our sport seek to improve the Rules under which we race. Every four years these alterations and improvements are incorporated in the Rules, which are then frozen for a further four year period. For the 1985–88 term the following amendments have been made:

The Rules now start with a paragraph about the Status of the Rules. With the increased number of cases in courts of law, which make reference to the IYR Rules, this statement has become necessary.

Notice there is now a clause added to the definition of Obstruction which allows the Sailing instructions to refer to certain areas as Obstructions or no-go-areas.

Where International events make use of national prescriptions English versions must be available for competitors.

In Rule 8 the old system of individual recall numbers displayed on boards has been removed.

Rule 26, this controversial rule has been modified yet again, under increasing pressure from some parts of the world, to allow greater advertising.

An important change is made with Rule 33.2 Contact between yachts racing. If there is 'minor and unavoidable contact' between yachts racing then a protest is no longer obligatory. Should a third yacht consider that the contact was indeed worse than 'minor and unavoidable', then he may protest. The decision is then in the hands of the Protest Committee. Should one of the colliding yachts wish to cover herself under 33.2 the com-

4

mittee may allow her to withdraw her protest under a new clause in Rule 68.9.

Rule 42 has been rewritten to make it, hopefully, easier to understand. The meaning is the same with the exception of Rule 42.3(a) (ii) which has been altered for clarification.

There is a new paragraph in Rule 43 dealing with an obstruction that is also a starting mark surrounded by navigable water. 43.3(a) has been put in to lessen the plight of the committee vessel. It's ground tackle is now part of the mark.

Rule 51.1(c) has been altered to remove reference to general recalls, and to mention the use of Code flag 'I'.

The Rule that describes the rounding or passing of marks, Rule 51.2, has been modified to stop those clever yachtsmen from cheating the course designers and cutting the corners.

In Part V there has been a major shuf-fle of rule numbers. Rule 58 has been repositioned as Fundamental Rule A.

With increasing worry of injuries to helmsmen and crews, the higher limit for weight of water-jackets has been deleted, while it is still not clear how to deal with the problem.

For the comfort of the offshore racing crewman Rule 62 has been modified to allow him to position his head and shoulders outside the upper lifeline.

Part VI is little changed. There are two additions to Rule 69; 69(c) expands on the disablement of a yacht, and 69(d) adds another circumstance under which a yacht may seek redress.

In the Appendices there are several additions. In Appendix 1 the IOC Eligibility Code has been included at the request of the IOC, and there is now an Appendix 11 dealing with Photographic Evidence.

THE 1985–88 INTERNATIONAL YACHT RACING RULES

© 1985 International Yacht Racing Union

International Yacht Racing Union
60 Knightsbridge
Westminster
London SW1X 7JX
England

CONTENTS

INTRODUCTION

Part I—STATUS OF THE RULES, FUNDAMENTAL RULES AND DEFINITIONS

Part II—MANAGEMENT OF RACES Authority and Duties of Race Committee

Part III—GENERAL REQUIREMENTS Owner's Responsibilities for Qualifying his Yacht

Contents

Introduction

Translation and Interpretation
In translating and interpreting these rules, it shall be understood that the word
"shall" is mandatory, and the words "can" and "may" are permissive.

Note (a) Marginal markings indicate the changes made in the 1981 Racing Rules.

Note (b) No changes are contemplated before 1989.

Note (c) These racing rules supersede all previous editions.

Note (d) In this issue, rule 58, Rendering Assistance, has been moved to become a
Fundamental Rule. Rule 55, Owner Steering another Yacht, becomes rule
20.3. Rules 22.3 and 28 have been moved to Part V, which has been
rearranged as follows:

New Rule		Old Rule
53	Casting Off, Anchoring, Making Fast and Hauling Out	63
54	Means of Propulsion	60
55	Aground or Foul of an Obstruction	64
56	Sounding	61
57	Manual and Stored Power	62
58	Boarding	56
59	Leaving, Crew Overboard	57
60	Outside Assistance	59
61	Clothing and Equipment	22.3
62	Increasing Stability	66
63	Skin Friction	65
64	Setting and Sheeting Sails	54
65	Flags	28
66	Fog Signals and Lights	53

Rules 50, 51 and 52 remain the same.

Part I—Status of the Rules, Fundamental Rules and Definitions

Status of the Rules

The International Yacht Racing Rules have been established by the International Yacht Racing Union for the organisation, conduct and judging of the sport of yacht racing, and are amended and published every four years by the IYRU in accordance with its Constitution.

A national authority may alter or add to these rules by prescription, with the exception of the rules of Parts I and IV and rules 1, 3, 26 and 61, unless permitted in a rule itself.

The sailing instructions may alter rules only in accordance with rule 3.1, (The Sailing Instructions).

Fundamental Rules

73
122

A. Rendering Assistance

Every yacht shall render all possible assistance to any vessel or person in peril, when in a position to do so.

73

B. Responsibility of a Yacht

It shall be the sole responsibility of each yacht to decide whether or not to *start* or to continue to *race*.

73
122

C. Fair Sailing

A yacht shall participate in a race or series of races in an event only by fair sailing, superior speed and skill, and, except in team races, by individual effort. However, a yacht may be penalised under this rule only in the case of a clear-cut violation of the above principles and only when no other rule (except rule 75, Gross Infringement of Rules or Misconduct) applies.

Definitions

When a term defined in Part I is used in its defined sense it is printed in **italic** *type. All preambles and definitions rank as rules. Further definitions of terms used in Part VI will be found at the beginning of Part VI.*

73

Racing—A yacht is *racing* from her preparatory signal until she has either *finished* and cleared the finishing line and finishing *marks* or retired, or until the race has been *postponed, abandoned, cancelled*, or a general recall has been signalled, except that in match or team races, the sailing instructions may prescribe that a yacht is *racing* from any specified time before the preparatory signal.

73
122
73
74
122

Starting—A yacht *starts* when, after fulfilling her penalty obligations, if any, under rule 51.1(c), (Sailing the Course), and after her starting signal, any part of her hull, crew or equipment first crosses the starting line in the direction of the course to the first *mark*.

Finishing—A yacht *finishes* when any part of her hull, or of her crew or equipment in normal position, crosses the finishing line in the direction of the course from the last *mark*, after fulfilling her penalty obligations, if any, under rule 52.2, (Touching a Mark).

Luffing—Altering course towards the wind.

Tacking—A yacht is *tacking* from the moment she is beyond head to wind until she has *borne away*, when beating to windward, to a *close-hauled* course; when not beating to windward, to the course on which her mainsail has filled.

Bearing Away—Altering course away from the wind until a yacht begins to *gybe*.

Gybing—A yacht begins to *gybe* at the moment when, with the wind aft, the foot of her mainsail crosses her centre line, and completes the *gybe* when the mainsail has filled on the other *tack*.

On a Tack—A yacht is *on a tack* except when she is *tacking* or *gybing*. A yacht is on the *tack* (*starboard* or *port*) corresponding to her *windward* side.

Close-hauled—A yacht is *close-hauled* when sailing by the wind as close as she can lie with advantage in working to windward.

Clear Astern and *Clear Ahead; Overlap*—A yacht is *clear astern* of another when her hull and equipment in normal position are abaft an imaginary line projected abeam from the aftermost point of the other's hull and equipment in normal position. The other yacht is *clear ahead*.

The yachts *overlap* when neither is *clear astern*; or when, although one is *clear astern*, an intervening yacht *overlaps* both of them.

The terms *clear astern, clear ahead* and *overlap* apply to yachts on opposite *tacks* only when they are subject to rule 42, (Rounding or Passing Marks and Obstructions).

Leeward and *Windward*—The *leeward* side of a yacht is that on which she is, or, when head to wind, was, carrying her mainsail. The opposite side is the *windward* side.

When neither of two yachts on the same *tack* is *clear astern*, the one on the *leeward* side of the other is the *leeward yacht*. The other is the *windward yacht*.

Proper Course—A *proper course* is any course that a yacht might sail after the starting signal, in the absence of the other yacht or yachts affected, to *finish* as quickly as possible. The course sailed before *luffing* or *bearing away* is presumably, but not necessarily, that yacht's *proper course*. There is no *proper course* before the starting signal.

Mark—A *mark* is any object specified in the sailing instructions that a yacht must round or pass on a required side.

Every ordinary part of a *mark* ranks as part of it, including a flag, flagpole, boom or hoisted boat, but excluding ground tackle and any object either accidentally or temporarily attached to the *mark*.

Obstruction—An *obstruction* is any object, including a vessel under way, large enough to require a yacht, when more than one overall length away from it, to make a substantial alteration of course to pass on one side or the other, or any object that can be passed on one side only, including a buoy when the yacht in question cannot safely pass between it and the shoal or object that it marks. The sailing instructions may prescribe that certain defined areas shall rank as *obstructions*.

Postponement—A *postponed* race is one that is not started at its scheduled time and that can be sailed at any time the race committee may decide.

Abandonment—An *abandoned* race is one that the race committee declares void at any time after the starting signal, and that can be re-sailed at its discretion.

Cancellation—A *cancelled* race is one that the race committee decides will not be sailed thereafter.

Part II—**Management of Races**

Authority and Duties of Race Committee

The rules of Part II deal with the duties and responsibilities of the race committee in conducting a race, the meaning of signals made by it and of other actions taken by it.

1 **Authority for Organising, Conducting and Judging Races**

1.1 Regattas and races shall be organised by either:
   (a) the I.Y.R.U.; or
   (b) a national authority recognised by the I.Y.R.U.; or
   (c) a club or regatta committee affiliated to a national authority; or
   (d) a class association either with the approval of a national authority or in conjunction with an affiliated club or regatta committee; or
   (e) an unaffiliated body in conjunction with an affiliated club or regatta committee,
   which will henceforth be referred to as the organising authority.

   All races shall be organised, conducted and judged under the rules of the I.Y.R.U. The organising authority shall appoint a race committee and publish the notice of race or regatta containing the terms and conditions of the event in accordance with rule 2, (Notice of Race or Regatta).

1.2 Subject to such direction as the organising authority may exercise, all races shall be conducted and judged by the race committee in conformity with the published terms and conditions. The term "race committee" whenever it is used shall include any person or committee that is responsible for carrying out any of the designated duties or functions of the race committee.

1.3 Unless otherwise prescribed by the national authority, the organising authority or the race committee may, before the start of a race or series, reject or rescind the entry of any yacht or exclude a competitor, without stating the reason. However, at all world and continental championships, no entry within established quotas shall be rejected or rescinded without first obtaining the approval of the I.Y.R.U. or the duly authorised international class association.

1.4 (a) The race committee and all other bodies and persons concerned with the organisation and conduct of the races or regatta shall be governed by these rules, by the prescriptions of its national authority when they apply, by the sailing instructions, by the class rules (except when they conflict with these rules) and, when applicable, by the Sailboard Racing Rules as contained in Appendix 2 or the Team Racing Rules as contained in Appendix 4, and shall decide all questions in accordance therewith.

   (b) The organising authority may modify class rules only for a race or regatta that is not subject to the control of that class association.

1.5 The receiving, initiating, hearing and deciding of protests and requests for redress shall be carried out either:

(a) by the race committee itself; or

(b) by a sub-committee thereof appointed by the race committee from its own members or from outside the committee or from a combination of them; or

(c) by a protest committee or a jury, separate from and independent of the race committee, appointed by the organising authority or the race committee; or

(d) by an international jury appointed by the organising authority in accordance with rule 1.6 and Appendix 8, (Terms of Reference of an International Jury and Conditions for its Decisions to be Final), that shall have supervision over the conduct of the races and power to direct the race committee, but only to the extent specifically provided in the terms and conditions of the regatta.

The term "jury", as used in yacht racing, means a panel of judges.

1.6   International juries may be appointed in accordance with rule 1.5(d):

(a) for the Olympic regatta and similar regattas open to yachts from different countries and in such other international regattas as are under the jurisdiction of the I.Y.R.U. or a national authority; or

(b) for international regattas under the jurisdiction of an international class association; or

(c) for international regattas not included in (a) or (b) when the organising authority so advises in the notice of race or regatta or in the sailing instructions.

1.7   The right of appeal may be denied only when either:

(a) an international jury is properly constituted, except that a national authority may prescribe that its approval is required for international juries appointed in accordance with rules 1.6(b) and (c); or

(b) it is essential to determine promptly the result of a race or series of races that will qualify a yacht to compete in a later stage of the event or a subsequent event. A national authority may prescribe that its approval be required for such a procedure; or

(c) a national authority so prescribes for a particular event open only to entries under its own jurisdiction.

When the right of appeal is to be denied, the organising authority shall announce its intention in the notice of race or regatta and in the sailing instructions.

2   Notice of Race or Regatta

The notice of a race or regatta shall contain the following information:

(a) The title, place and dates of the event and name of the organising authority.

(b) That the race or regatta will be governed by the International Yacht Racing Rules, the prescriptions of the national authority when they apply (for international events, a copy in English of prescriptions that apply shall be available to each yacht), the rules of each class concerned; and such other rules as are applicable. When class rules are modified in accordance with rule 1.4(b), the modifications shall be stated.

(c) The class(es) to race, conditions of eligibility or entry and, when appropriate, restrictions on numbers of entries.

(d) The times of registration and starts of the practice race or first race, and succeeding races when known.

The notice shall, when appropriate, include the following:

(e) The scoring system.

(f) The time and place at which the sailing instructions will be available.

(g) Variations from the racing rules, subject to rule 3.1. (The Sailing Instructions).

(h) The procedure for advance registration or entry, including closing dates when applicable, fees and the mailing address.

(i) Measurement procedures or requirements for measuring or rating certificates.

(j) The course(s) to be sailed.

(k) Alternative penalties for rule infringements.

(l) Prizes.

(m)Denial of the right to appeal, subject to rule 1.7.

3   The Sailing Instructions

3.1   STATUS
These rules shall be supplemented by written sailing instructions which shall rank as rules and may alter a rule by specific reference to it, but, except in accordance with rule 3.2 (b) (xxviii), they shall not alter Parts I and IV of these rules, or rules 1, 2, 3, 26, 51.1 (a) or 61, or the rules of Sections C and D of Part VI, or the provision of rule 68.2(a), (Protests by Yachts), that International Code flag "B" is always acceptable as a protest flag. However, when so prescribed by the national authority, this restriction shall not preclude the right of developing and testing proposed rule changes in local regattas.

123

3.2   CONTENTS

(a) The sailing instructions shall contain the following information:

78
79

(i)   That the race or regatta will be governed by the International Yacht Racing Rules, the prescriptions of the national authority when they apply (for international events, a copy in English of prescriptions that apply shall be included in the sailing instructions), the rules of each class concerned, the sailing instructions and such other rules as are applicable.

(ii)   The schedule of races, the classes to race, and the order and times of warning signals.

(iii)   The course or courses to be sailed or a list of *marks* or courses from which the course or courses will be selected, describing the *marks* and stating:

1 the order, and either

2 the side on which each *mark* is to be rounded, or

3 the side on which each *mark* is to be passed.

A diagram or chart is recommended.

(iv) Description of the starting line, the starting system and any special signals to be used.

(v) The procedure for individual and general recalls and any special signals.

(vi) Description of the finishing line and any special instructions for *finishing* a course shortened after the start.

(vii) The time limit, if any, for *finishing*.

(viii) The scoring system, when not previously announced in writing, including the method, if any, for breaking ties.

(b) The sailing instructions shall, when appropriate, include the following:

(i) Variations from the racing rules, subject to rule 3.1, or the class rules for a special race or regatta.

(ii) The registration procedure.

(iii) Location(s) of official regatta notice board(s).

(iv) Procedure for changes in the sailing instructions.

(v) Restrictions controlling modifications to yachts when supplied by the organising authority.

(vi) Signals to be made ashore and location of signal station(s).

(vii) Class flags.

(viii) The racing area. A chart is recommended.

(ix) The starting area.

(x) Course signals.

(xi) Approximate course length; approximate length of windward legs.

(xii) Information on tides and currents.

(xiii) Procedure for shortening the course before or after the start.

(xiv) Mark boats; lead boats.

(xv) Procedure for changes of course after the start and related signals.

(xvi) The time limit, if any, for yachts other than the first yacht to finish.

(xvii) Whether races *postponed* or *abandoned* for the day will be sailed later and, if so, when and where.

(xviii) The number of races required to complete the regatta.

(xix) Safety, such as requirements and signals for personal buoyancy, check-in at the starting area, and check-out and check-in ashore.

(xx) Any measurement or inspection procedure.

(xxi) Alternative penalties for rule infringements.

(xxii) Whether declarations are required.

(xxiii) Protest procedure and times and place of hearings.

(xxiv) Restrictions on use of support boats, plastic pools, radios, etc. and limitations on hauling out.

    (xxv) Substitute competitors.

    (xxvi) Prizes.

    (xxvii) Time allowances.

    (xxviii)Racing rules applicable between sunset and sunrise and night signals to be used by the race committee.

    (xxix) Disposition to be made of a yacht appearing at the start alone in her class.

    (xxx) Denial of the right to appeal, subject to rule 1.7.

    (xxxi) Other commitments of the race committee and obligations of yachts.

3.3 DISTRIBUTION
The sailing instructions shall be available to each yacht entitled to *race*.

3.4 CHANGES
Before a race or during a series, the race committee may change the sailing instructions by timely posting a written notice on the official notice board. On the water, it may make such a change by communicating it to each yacht before her warning signal.

3.5 ORAL INSTRUCTIONS
Oral instructions shall not be given, except in accordance with procedure specifically set out in the sailing instructions.

4 Signals

4.1 VISUAL SIGNALS
Unless otherwise prescribed in the sailing instructions, the following International Code flags (or boards) and other visual signals shall be used as indicated and when displayed alone shall apply to all classes, and when displayed over a class signal they shall apply to the designated class only:

"AP", Answering Pendant — Postponement Signal

Means:

    (a) "All races not started are *postponed*. The warning signal will be made one minute after this signal is lowered."
        (One sound signal shall be made with the lowering of the "AP".)

    (b) Over one ball or shape.
        "The scheduled starting times of all races not started are *postponed* fifteen minutes."
        (This *postponement* can be extended indefinitely by the addition of one ball or shape for every fifteen minutes.)

    (c) Over one of the numeral pendants 1 to 9.
        "All races not started are *postponed* one hour, two hours, etc."

    (d) Over Code flag "A".
        "All races not started are *postponed* to a later day."

"B" — Protest signal.

    When displayed by a yacht.
    Means:
    "I intend to lodge a protest."

"C" — Change of Course while Racing.

When displayed at or near a rounding *mark*.
Means:
"After rounding this *mark*, the course to the next *mark* has been changed."

"I" — Round the Ends Starting Rule.

Displayed before or with the preparatory signal.
Means:
"Rule 51.1(c) will be in effect for this start."
When lowered, accompanied by one long sound signal, one minute before the starting signal.
Means:
"The one-minute period of rule 51.1(c) has begun."

"L" — Means:

(a) When displayed ashore:
"A notice to competitors has been posted on the notice board."

(b) When displayed afloat:
"Come within hail," or "Follow me."

"M" — Mark Signal.

When displayed on a buoy, vessel, or other object.
Means:
"Round or pass the object displaying this signal instead of the *mark* that it replaces."

"N" — Abandonment Signal.

Means:
"All races are *abandoned*."

"N over X" — Abandonment and Re-sail Signal.

Means:
"All races are *abandoned* and will shortly be re-sailed. The warning signal will be made one minute after this signal is lowered."
(One sound signal shall be made with the lowering of "N over X".)

"N over First Substitute" — Cancellation Signal.

Means:
"All races are *cancelled*."

"P" — Preparatory Signal.

Means:
"The class designated by the warning signal will *start* in five minutes exactly."

"S" — Shorten Course Signal.

Means:

(a) at the starting line:
"Sail the shortened course prescribed in the sailing instructions."

(b) at the finishing line:
"*Finish* the race either:
(i) at the prescribed finishing line at the end of the round still to be completed by the leading yacht, or
(ii) as prescribed in the sailing instructions."

(c) at a rounding *mark*:
"*Finish* between the rounding *mark* and the committee boat."

"X" — Individual Recall.

> Broken out immediately after the starting signal is made, accompanied by one sound signal, in accordance with rule 8.1(a)(ii), (Recalls).
> Means:
> "One or more yachts have started prematurely or have infringed the Round the Ends Starting Rule 51.1(c)."

"Y" — Life Jacket Signal.

> Means:
> "Life jackets or other adequate personal buoyancy shall be worn while *racing* by all helmsmen and crews, unless specifically excepted in the sailing instructions."
> When this signal is displayed after the warning signal is made, failure to comply shall not be cause for disqualification.
> Notwithstanding anything in this rule, it shall be the individual responsibility of each competitor to wear a life jacket or other adequate personal buoyancy when conditions warrant. A wet suit is not adequate personal buoyancy.

"First Substitute" — General Recall Signal.

> Means:
> "The class is recalled for a new start as provided in the sailing instructions."
> Unless the sailing instructions prescribe some other signal, the warning signal will be made one minute after this signal is lowered. (One sound signal shall be made with the lowering of "First Substitute".)

Red Flag — Displayed by committee boat.

> Means:
> "Leave all marks to port."

Green Flag — Displayed by committee boat.

> Means:
> "Leave all marks to starboard."

Blue Flag or Shape — Finishing Signal.

> When displayed by a committee boat.
> Means:
> "The committee boat is on station at the finishing line."

4.2   SIGNALS FOR STARTING A RACE

(a) Unless otherwise prescribed in the sailing instructions, the signals for starting a race shall be made at five-minute intervals exactly, and shall be either:

System 1	Warning Signal	— Class flag broken out or distinctive signal displayed.
	Preparatory Signal	— Code flag "P" broken out or distinctive signal displayed.
	Starting Signal	— Both warning and preparatory signals lowered.

In System 1, when classes are started:

(i)   at ten-minute intervals—
the warning signal for each succeeding class shall be broken out or displayed at the starting signal of the preceding class.

(ii) at five-minute intervals—
the preparatory signal for the first class to start shall be left displayed until the last class starts. The warning signal for each succeeding class shall be broken out or displayed at the preparatory signal of the preceding class.

or

System 2   Warning Signal — White or yellow shape.

Preparatory Signal — Blue shape.

Starting Signal for — Red shape.
first class to start

In System 2, each signal shall be lowered one minute before the next is made.
Class flags when used shall be broken out not later than the preparatory signal for each class.
In starting a series of classes:

(i) at ten-minute intervals—
the starting signal for each class shall be the warning signal for the next.

(ii) at five-minute intervals—
the preparatory signal for each class shall be the the the warning signal for the next.

(b) Although rules 4.1 "P" and 4.2(a) specify five-minute intervals between signals, the sailing instructions may prescribe any intervals.

(c) A warning signal shall not be made before its scheduled time, except with the consent of all yachts entitled to *race*.

(d) When a significant error is made in the timing of the interval between any of the signals for starting a race, the recommended procedure is to signal a general recall, *postponement* or *abandonment* of the race whose start is directly affected by the error and a corresponding *postponement* of succeeding races. Unless otherwise prescribed in the sailing instructions, a new warning signal shall be made. When the race is not recalled, *postponed* or *abandoned* after an error in the timing of the interval, each succeeding signal shall be made at the correct interval from the preceding signal.

79

4.3   OTHER SIGNALS
The sailing instructions shall designate any other special signals and shall explain their meaning.

79

4.4   CALLING ATTENTION TO SIGNALS
Whenever the race committee makes a signal, except "S" before the warning signal or a blue flag or shape when on station at the finishing line, it shall call attention to its action as follows:

(a) Three guns or other sound signals when displaying:

(i) "N";

(ii) "N over X";

(iii) "N over First Substitute".

(b) Two guns or other sound signals when displaying:

(i) "AP";

        (ii)   "S";

        (iii)   "First Substitute".

(c) Repetitive sound signals while displaying Code flag "C".

(d) One gun or other sound signal when making any other signal, including the lowering of:

        (i)   "AP" when the length of the postponement is not signalled;

        (ii)   "N over X";

        (iii)   "First Substitute".

79
124

4.5 VISUAL STARTING SIGNALS TO GOVERN

Times shall be taken from the visual starting signals, and a failure or mistiming of a gun or other sound signal calling attention to starting signals shall be disregarded.

5 **Designating the Course, Altering the Course or Race**

5.1 Before or with the warning signal for a class that has not *started*, the race committee:

(a) shall either signal or otherwise designate the course.

124

(b) may remove and substitute a new course signal.

5.2 Before the preparatory signal, the race committee may shift a starting *mark*.

5.3 Before the starting signal, the race committee may:

(a) shorten the course to one prescribed in the sailing instructions.

(b) *postpone* to designate a new course before or with the new warning signal, or for any other reason.

(c) *postpone* to a later day.

(d) *cancel* the race for any reason.

5.4 After the starting signal, the race committee may:

(a) *abandon* and resail the race when there is an error in starting procedure.

(b) change the course at any rounding *mark* subject to proper notice being given to each yacht as prescribed in the sailing instructions.

(c) shorten the course by finishing a race at any rounding *mark* or as prescribed in the sailing instructions, or *abandon* or *cancel* the race:

        (i)   because of foul weather endangering the yachts, or

        (ii)   because of insufficient wind making it improbable that the race will finish within the time limit, or

        (iii)   because a *mark* is missing or has shifted, or

        (iv)   for any other reasons (other than changes in the weather conditions) directly affecting the safety or fairness of the competition.

5.5 After a race has been completed, the race committee shall not *abandon* or *cancel* it without taking the appropriate action under rule 74.2(b), (Consideration of Redress).

5.6 The race committee shall notify all yachts concerned by signal or otherwise when and where a race *postponed* to a later day or *abandoned* will be sailed.

6   Starting and Finishing Lines

The starting and finishing lines shall be either:

(a) a line between a *mark* and a mast or staff on the committee boat or station clearly identified in the sailing instructions; or

(b) a line between two *marks*; or

(c) the extension of a line through two stationary posts, with or without a *mark* at or near its outer limit, inside which the yachts shall pass.

For types (a) and (c) of starting or finishing lines the sailing instructions may also prescribe that a *mark* will be laid at or near the inner end of the line, in which case yachts shall pass between it and the outer *mark*.

7   Start of a Race

7.1   STARTING AREA
The sailing instructions may define a starting area that may be bounded by buoys; if so, they shall not rank as *marks*.

7.2   TIMING THE START
The *start* of a yacht shall be timed from her starting signal.

8   Recalls

8.1   INDIVIDUAL RECALL
When, at her starting signal, any part of a yacht's hull, crew or equipment is on the course side of the starting line or its extensions, or she is subject to rule 51.1(c), (Sailing the Course), the race committee shall:

either

(a) make a suitable sound signal and either:

(i)   lower the class warning signal to "the dip"; or

(ii)   display Code flag "X"
until all such yachts are wholly on the pre-start side of the starting line or its extensions, or for four minutes after the starting signal, whichever is the earlier; or

(iii)   hail her sail number.

The sailing instructions shall prescribe which of these options will apply.

or

(b) follow such other procedure as may be prescribed in the sailing instructions.

8.2   GENERAL RECALL

(a) When there is either a number of unidentified premature starters or an error in starting procedure, the race committee may make a general recall signal in accordance with rules 4.1, ("First Substitute"), and 4.4, (Calling Attention to Signals). Unless otherwise prescribed in the sailing instructions, new warning and preparatory signals shall be made.

(b) Except as provided in rule 31.2, (Disqualification), rule infringements before the preparatory signal for the new start shall be disregarded for the purpose of competing in the race to be re-started.

9   Marks

9.1   MARK MISSING

(a) When any *mark* either is missing or has shifted, the race committee shall, when possible, replace it in its stated position, or substitute a new one with similar characteristics or a buoy or vessel displaying Code flag "M"— the *mark* signal.

(b) When it is impossible either to replace the *mark* or to substitute a new one in time for the yachts to round or pass it, the race committee may, at its discretion, act in accordance with rule 5.4(c)(iii), (Designating the Course, Altering the Course or Race).

9.2   MARK UNSEEN

When races are sailed in fog or at night, dead reckoning alone need not necessarily be accepted as evidence that a *mark* has been rounded or passed.

10   Finishing Within a Time Limit

Unless otherwise prescribed in the sailing instructions, in races where there is a time limit, one yacht *finishing* within the prescribed limit shall make the race valid for all other yachts in that race.

11   Ties

When there is a tie at the finish of a race, either actual or on corrected times, the points for the place for which the yachts have tied and for the place immediately below shall be added together and divided equally. When two or more yachts tie for a trophy or prize in either a single race or a series, the yachts so tied shall, when practicable, sail a deciding race; if not, either the tie shall be broken by a method established under rule 3.2(a)(viii), (The Sailing Instructions), or the yachts so tied shall either receive equal prizes or share the prize.

12   Races to be Re-sailed

When a race is to be re-sailed:

(a) All yachts entered in the original race shall be eligible to *start* in the race to be re-sailed.

(b) Subject to the entry requirements of the original race, and at the discretion of the race committee, new entries may be accepted.

(c) Rule infringements in the original race shall be disregarded for the purpose of competing in the race to be re-sailed.

(d) The race committee shall notify the yachts concerned when and where the race will be re-sailed.

13   Award of Prizes

Before awarding the prizes, the race committee shall be satisfied that all yachts whose finishing positions affect the awards have observed the racing rules, the prescriptions of the national authority when they apply, the sailing instructions and the class rules.

(Numbers 14, 15, 16 and 17 are spare numbers)

Part III—**General Requirements**

Owner's Responsibilities for Qualifying his Yacht

A yacht intending to **race** *shall, to avoid subsequent disqualification, comply with the rules of Part III before her preparatory signal and, when applicable, while* **racing**.

18   Entries

Unless otherwise prescribed either in the notice of race or regatta or in the sailing instructions, entries shall be made in the following form:

FORM OF ENTRY

To the Secretary .... *Club*   **124**
    Please enter the yacht .... *for*
the .... *race, on the*..
her national letters and sail number are ....
her rig is ....
the colour of her hull is ....
and her rating or class is ....

    I agree to be bound by the racing rules of the I.Y.R.U., by the prescriptions of the national authority under which this race is sailed, by the sailing instructions and by the class rules.

                        Name ....
                        Address ....
                        Telephone No ....
                        Club ....
                        Address during event ....
                        Telephone No ....

Signed.. *Date*..
    (Owner or owner's representative)
Entrance fee enclosed

19   Measurement or Rating Certificates

19.1   Every yacht entering a race shall hold such valid measurement or rating certificate as required by the national authority or other duly authorised body, by her class rules, by the notice of race or regatta, or by the sailing instructions.

80

19.2   An owner shall be responsible for maintaining his yacht in accordance with her class rules and for ensuring that her certificate is not invalidated by alterations. Deviations in excess of tolerances specified in the class rules caused by normal wear or damage and that do not affect the performance of the yacht shall not invalidate the measurement or rating certificate of the yacht for a particular race, but shall be rectified before she *races* again, unless in the opinion of the race committee there has been no practicable opportunity to rectify the wear or damage.

19.3   (a) The owner of a yacht who cannot produce such a certificate when required, may be permitted to sign and lodge with the race committee, before she *starts*, a statement in the following form:

To the Secretary .... *Club*

UNDERTAKING TO PRODUCE CERTIFICATE

The yacht .... *competes in the* ....
*race on condition that a valid certificate previously issued by the authorised
administrative body, or a true copy of it, is submitted to the race committee
before the end of the series, and that she competes in the race(s) on the
measurement or rating of that certificate.*

> *Signed* ....
> *(Owner or his representative)*
> *Date* ....

(b) In this event the sailing instructions may require that the owner shall
lodge such a deposit as may be required by the organising authority,
which may be forfeited when such certificate or true copy is not
submitted to the race committee within the prescribed period.

20   Ownership of Yachts

20.1   Unless otherwise prescribed in the conditions of entry, a yacht shall be
eligible to compete only when she is either owned by or on charter to and
has been entered by a yacht or sailing club recognised by its national
authority or a member or members thereof.

20.2   Two or more yachts owned or chartered wholly or in part by the same body
or person shall not compete in the same race without the previous consent
of the race committee.

20.3   An owner shall not steer any yacht other than his own in a race wherein his
own yacht competes without the previous consent of the race committee.

21   Member on Board

Every yacht shall have on board a member of a yacht or sailing club
recognised by its national authority to be in charge of the yacht as owner or
owner's representative.

22   Shifting Ballast

22.1   GENERAL RESTRICTIONS
Floorboards shall be kept down; bulkheads and doors left standing; ladders,
stairways and water tanks left in place; all cabin, galley and forecastle
fixtures and fittings kept on board; all movable ballast shall be properly
stowed under the floorboards or in lockers and no dead weight shall be
shifted.

22.2   SHIPPING, UNSHIPPING OR SHIFTING BALLAST; WATER
From 2100 on the day before the race until she is no longer *racing*, a yacht
shall not ship, unship or shift ballast, whether movable or fixed, or take in or
discharge water, except for ordinary ship's use and the removal of bilge
water.

23   Anchor

Unless otherwise prescribed by her class rules, every yacht shall carry on
board an anchor and chain or rope of suitable size.

24   Life-Saving Equipment

Unless otherwise prescribed by her class rules, every yacht, except one that
has sufficient buoyancy to support the crew in case of accident, shall carry
adequate life-saving equipment for all persons on board, one item of which
shall be ready for immediate use.

25   **Class Insignia, National Letters and Sail Numbers**

25.1 Every yacht of an international class recognised by the I.Y.R.U. shall carry on her mainsail, and as provided in rule 25.1(d)(iii) on her spinnaker:

(a) The insignia denoting the class to which she belongs.

(b) A letter or letters showing her nationality, thus:

A	Argentina	GU	Guatemala	OE	Austria
AE	Dubai	H	Holland	OM	Oman
AN	Angola	I	Italy	P	Portugal
ANU	Antigua	IL	Iceland	PH	Philippines
AR	Egypt	IND	India	PK	Pakistan
B	Belgium	IR	Ireland	PR	Puerto Rico
BA	Bahamas	IS	Israel	PU	Peru
BL	Brazil	J	Japan	PY	Paraguay
BN	Brunei	K	United	PZ	Poland
BR	Burma		Kingdom	Q	Kuwait
BU	Bulgaria	KA	Australia	RB	Botswana
CB	Colombia	KB	Bermuda	RC	Cuba
CH	China	KBA	Barbados	RI	Indonesia
CI	Grand Cayman	KC	Canada	RM	Roumania
CP	Cyprus	KF	Fiji	S	Sweden
CR	Costa Rica	KH	Hong Kong	SA	South Africa
CY	Sri Lanka	KJ	Jamaica	SE	Senegal
CZ	Czechoslovakia	KK	Kenya	SK	Republic of
D	Denmark	KP	Papua New		Korea
DDR	German		Guinea	SM	San Marino
	Democratic	KS	Singapore	SR	Union of
	Republic	KT	Trinidad		Soviet Socialist
DK	Democratic		and Tobago		Republics
	People's Republic	KV	British	TA	Taipei
	of Korea		Virgin Is.	TH	Thailand
DR	Dominican	KZ	New Zealand	TK	Turkey
	Republic	L	Finland	U	Uruguay
E	Spain	LX	Luxembourg	US	United States
EC	Ecuador	M	Hungary		of America
F	France	MA	Morocco	V	Venezuela
FL	Liechtenstein	MO	Monaco	VI	U.S. Virgin Is.
G	Federal	MT	Malta	X	Chile
	Republic of	MX	Mexico	Y	Yugoslavia
	Germany	MY	Malaysia	Z	Switzerland
GR	Greece	N	Norway	ZB	Zimbabwe

(c) A sail number allotted to her by her national authority. In the case of a self-administered international class, the number may be allotted by the class owners' association.
National letters shall be placed in front of or above the sail numbers. When the national letters end in "I" (e.g. Italy, U.S. Virgin Islands) and are placed in front of the numbers, they shall be separated from them by a horizontal line approximately 50 mm long.

(d)   (i)   Unless otherwise prescribed in the class rules, the class insignia, national letter(s) and sail numbers shall be above an imaginary line projecting at right angles to the luff from a point one-third of the distance, measured from the tack, to the head of the sail; shall be clearly visible; and shall be placed at different heights on the two sides of the sail, those on the starboard side being uppermost.

(ii)   Where the class insignia is of such a design that, when placed back to back on the two sides of the sail, they coincide, they may be so placed.

(iii)   The national letters and sail numbers only shall be similarly placed on both sides of the spinnaker, but at approximately half-height.

(e) National letters need not be carried in home waters, except in an international championship.

(f) The following minimum sizes for national letters and sail numbers are prescribed:

Height: one-tenth of the measurement of the foot of the mainsail rounded up to the nearest 50 mm.

Width: (excluding number 1 and letter I) 66% of the height.

Thickness: 15% of the height.

Space between adjoining letters and numbers: 20% of the height.

Classes that have a variable sail plan shall specify in their class rules the sizes of letters and numbers, which shall, when practicable, conform to the above requirements.

25.2   Other yachts shall comply with the rules of their national authority or class in regard to the allottment, carrying and size of insignia, letters and numbers, which rules shall, when practicable, conform to the above requirements.

25.3   When so prescribed in the notice of race or regatta or the sailing instructions, a yacht chartered or loaned for an event may carry national letters or sail numbers in contravention of her class rules. In all other respects the sails shall comply with the class rules.

25.4   A yacht shall not be disqualified for infringing the provisions of rule 25 without prior warning and adequate opportunity to make correction.

26   Advertising

Rule 26 shall apply when *racing* and, in addition, unless otherwise prescribed in the notice of race or regatta, from 0700 on the first race day of a regatta or series until the expiry of the time limit for lodging protests following the last race of the regatta or series.

26.1   BASIC RULE
Unless permitted in accordance with rules 26.2 or 26.3, no advertising shall be displayed on the hull, spars, sails and equipment of a yacht while rule 26 is in effect, or on the clothing and equipment worn by the crew when the yacht is under way, except that:

(a) one sailmaker's mark (which may include the name or mark of the manufacturer of the sail cloth and pattern or model description of the sail) may be displayed on each side of any sail. The whole of such a mark shall be placed not more than 15% of the length of the foot of the sail or 300 mm from its tack, whichever is the greater. This latter limitation shall not apply to the position of marks on spinnakers.

(b) one builder's mark (which may include the name or mark of the designer) may be placed on the hull, and one maker's mark may be displayed on spars and equipment.

(c) such marks (or plates) shall fit within a square not exceeding 150 mm x 150 mm.

(d) one maker's mark may be displayed on each item of clothing and equipment worn by the crew, provided that the mark fits within a square not exceeding 100 mm x 100 mm.

(e) the yacht's type may be displayed once on each side of the hull, provided that the lettering shall not exceed 1% in height and 5% in length of the overall length of the yacht, but not exceeding a maximum height of 100 mm and a maximum length of 700 mm.

(f) a sailboard's type may be displayed on the hull in two places. The lettering shall not exceed 200 mm in height.

26.2   EXEMPTION FOR YACHTS
When a national authority wishes to permit further limited advertising, it shall prescribe that this exemption may be used, except that it shall not be granted to yachts in world and continental events and, unless so prescribed by the class rules, in the events of international classes.

(a) When the national authority gives written consent to a yacht, and when the yacht is sailing in its home waters:

    (i)   her name may be the name, product name or logo of a company or other organisation. The name shall not be displayed more than once on each side of the hull and on the transom, and shall not exceed in height 1½% and in length 10% of the overall length of the yacht, but not exceeding a maximum height of 300 mm and a maximum length of 2100 mm;

    (ii)   the name, product name or logo of the company or other organisation may be displayed on the clothing and equipment worn by the crew of the yacht.

(b) In giving such consent, the national authority:

    (i)   may limit the consent to one event or a series of events,

    (ii)   may limit the duration of its validity,

    (iii)   shall reserve the right to withdraw such consent, and

    (iv)   may impose such other terms as it sees fit.

(c) The letter of consent shall be displayed for the duration of an event on the official regatta notice board. When the letter of consent is not displayed, the consent shall be invalid.

(d) When a yacht is granted the exemption in rule 26.2 by her national authority, another national authority may also give consent in accordance with rule 26.2 to the yacht when she is sailing in its waters.

26.3   EXEMPTION FOR EVENTS
When authorised by a national authority for an event in its home waters for which all yachts will be supplied by a company or other organisation, the organising authority may permit advertising on the hull of the yachts within the dimensional limitations of rule 26.2(a)(i), and in two places on one boom. However, a competitor shall not be required or induced to display advertising on his clothing or equipment.

26.4   DISPENSATION
When a national authority is satisfied, before an event begins, that yachts *raced* with advertising in the same event prior to 16th November, 1983, it may consent to dispensation from part or all of rule 26. In such case, the

organising authority shall obtain written approval from the national authority, and that approval shall be announced in the notice of race or regatta and in the sailing instructions.

26.5 WARNING AND PENALTIES
As an alternative from or in addition to the penalties prescribed by rule 74.4, (Penalties), the race committee may:

(a) warn the infringing yacht that a further infringement will result in action under rule 70.2, (Action by Race or Protest Committee).

(b) when the infringement occurs when the yacht is not *racing*, disqualify the yacht from the race most recently sailed or from the next race sailed after the infringement.

(c) when it decides there was a gross breach of this rule, disqualify the yacht from more than one race or from the whole series.

27 Forestays and Jib Tacks

Unless otherwise prescribed by the class rules, forestays and jib tacks (not including spinnaker staysails when not *close-hauled*) shall be fixed approximately in the centre-line of the yacht.

(Numbers 28, 29 and 30 are spare numbers)

Part IV—**Right of Way Rules**

Rights and Obligations when Yachts Meet

*The rules of Part IV do not apply in any way to a vessel that is neither intending to **race** nor **racing**; such vessel shall be treated in accordance with the International Regulations for Preventing Collisions at Sea or Government Right of Way Rules applicable to the area concerned. The rules of Part IV apply only between yachts that either are intending to **race** or are **racing** in the same or different races, and, except when rule 3.2(b)(xxviii), (Race Continues After Sunset), applies, replace the International Regulations for Preventing Collisions at Sea or Government Right of Way Rules applicable to the area concerned, from the time a yacht intending to **race** begins to sail about in the vicinity of the starting line until she has either **finished** or retired and has left the vicinity of the course. (See Appendix 9).*

SECTION A—**Obligations and Penalties**

31   Disqualification   **81**

31.1   A yacht may be disqualified or otherwise penalised for infringing a rule of Part IV only when the infringement occurs while she is *racing*, whether or not a collision results.

31.2   A yacht may be disqualified or otherwise penalised, before or after she is *racing*, for seriously hindering a yacht that is *racing* or for infringing the sailing instructions.

32   Avoiding Collisions   **81**
                                                                                   124
A right-of-way yacht that fails to make a reasonable attempt to avoid a   **125**
collision resulting in serious damage may be disqualified as well as the other
yacht.

33   Rule Infringement

33.1   ACCEPTING PENALTY   **81**
A yacht that realises she has infringed a racing rule or a sailing instruction is **125**
under an obligation either to retire promptly or to exonerate herself by
accepting an alternative penalty when so prescribed in the sailing instructions, but when she does not retire or exonerate herself and persists in
racing, other yachts shall continue to accord her such rights as she has
under the rules of Part IV.

33.2   CONTACT BETWEEN YACHTS RACING
When there is contact that is not both minor and unavoidable between the
hulls, equipment or crew of two yachts, both shall be disqualified or
otherwise penalised unless:

either

(a) one of the yachts retires in acknowledgement of the infringement, or
    exonerates herself by accepting an alternative penalty when so pre-
    scribed in the sailing instructions,

or

(b) one or both of these yachts acts in accordance with rule 68, (Protests by Yachts).

34   Hailing

82
125

34.1   Except when *luffing* under rule 38.1, (Luffing and Sailing above a Proper Course after Starting), a right-of-way yacht that does not hail before or when making an alteration of course that may not be foreseen by the other yacht may be disqualified as well as the yacht required to keep clear when a collision resulting in serious damage occurs.

34.2   A yacht that hails when claiming the establishment or termination of an *overlap* or insufficiency of room at a *mark* or *obstruction* thereby helps to support her claim for the purposes of rule 42, (Rounding or Passing Marks and Obstructions).

SECTION B—Principal Right of Way Rules and their Limitations

These rules apply except when over-ridden by a rule in Section C.

35   Limitations on Altering Course

82
83
84
125

When one yacht is required to keep clear of another, the right-of-way yacht shall not alter course so as to prevent the other yacht from keeping clear; or so as to obstruct her while she is keeping clear, except:

(a) to the extent permitted by rule 38.1, (Same Tack, Luffing and Sailing above a Proper Course after Starting), and

(b) when assuming a *proper course*:
either

(i)   to *start*, unless subject to rule 40, (Same Tack, Luffing before Starting), or to the second part of rule 44.1(b), (Returning to Start),

or

(ii)   when rounding a *mark*.

84
85

36   Opposite Tacks—Basic Rule

A *port-tack* yacht shall keep clear of a *starboard-tack* yacht.

92
85
86

37   Same Tack—Basic Rules

37.1   WHEN OVERLAPPED
A *windward yacht* shall keep clear of a *leeward yacht*.

37.2   WHEN NOT OVERLAPPED
A yacht *clear astern* shall keep clear of a yacht *clear ahead*.

37.3   TRANSITIONAL
A yacht that establishes an *overlap* to *leeward* from *clear astern* shall allow the *windward yacht* ample room and opportunity to keep clear.

38 Same Tack—Luffing and Sailing above a Proper Course after Starting

38.1 LUFFING RIGHTS

After she has *started* and cleared the starting line, a yacht *clear ahead* or a *leeward yacht* may *luff* as she pleases, subject to the *proper course* limitations of this rule.

87

38.2 PROPER COURSE LIMITATIONS

A *leeward yacht* shall not sail above her *proper course* while an *overlap* exists, if when the *overlap* began or at any time during its existence, the helmsman of the *windward yacht* (when sighting abeam from his normal station and sailing no higher than the *leeward yacht*) has been abreast or forward of the mainmast of the *leeward yacht*.

87

38.3 OVERLAP LIMITATIONS

For the purpose of rule 38 only: An *overlap* does not exist unless the yachts are clearly within two overall lengths of the longer yacht; and an *overlap* that exists between two yachts when the leading yacht *starts*, or when one or both of them completes a *tack* or *gybe*, shall be regarded as a new *overlap* beginning at that time.

88
89

38.4 HAILING TO STOP OR PREVENT A LUFF

When there is doubt, the *leeward yacht* may assume that she has the right to *luff* unless the helmsman of the *windward yacht* has hailed "Mast Abeam", or words to that effect. The *leeward yacht* shall be governed by such hail, and, when she deems it improper, her only remedy is to protest.

90

38.5 CURTAILING A LUFF

The *windward yacht* shall not cause a *luff* to be curtailed because of her proximity to the *leeward yacht* unless an *obstruction*, a third yacht or other object restricts her ability to respond.

91

38.6 LUFFING TWO OR MORE YACHTS

A yacht shall not *luff* unless she has the right to *luff* all yachts that would be affected by her *luff*, in which case they shall all respond, even when an intervening yacht or yachts would not otherwise have the right to *luff*.

91

39 Same Tack—Sailing below a Proper Course after Starting

A yacht that is on a free leg of the course shall not sail below her *proper course* when she is clearly within three of her overall lengths of either a *leeward yacht* or a yacht *clear astern* that is steering a course to pass to leeward.

92

40 Same Tack—Luffing before Starting

Before a right-of-way yacht has *started* and cleared the starting line, any *luff* on her part that causes another yacht to have to alter course to avoid a collision shall be carried out slowly and initially in such a way as to give a *windward yacht* room and opportunity to keep clear. However, the *leeward yacht* shall not so *luff* above a *close-hauled* course, unless the helmsman of the *windward yacht* (sighting abeam from his normal station) is abaft the mainmast of the *leeward yacht*. Rules 38.4, (Hailing to Stop or Prevent a Luff); 38.5, (Curtailing a Luff); and 38.6, (Luffing Two or more Yachts), also apply.

93

41 Changing Tacks—Tacking and Gybing

41.1 BASIC RULE

A yacht that is either *tacking* or *gybing* shall keep clear of a yacht *on a tack*.

94

41.2   TRANSITIONAL
A yacht shall neither *tack* nor *gybe* into a position that will give her right of way, unless she does so far enough from a yacht *on a tack* to enable this yacht to keep clear without having to begin to alter her course until after the *tack* or *gybe* has been completed.

41.3   ONUS
A yacht that *tacks* or *gybes* has the onus of satisfying the race committee that she completed her *tack* or *gybe* in accordance with rule 41.2.

41.4   WHEN SIMULTANEOUS
When two yachts are both *tacking* or both *gybing* at the same time, the one on the other's port side shall keep clear.

SECTION C—Rules that Apply at Marks and Obstructions and other Exceptions to the Rules of Section B

When a rule of this section applies, to the extent to which it explicitly provides rights and obligations, it over-rides any conflicting rule of Section B, Principal Right of Way Rules and their Limitations, except rule 35, (Limitations on Altering Course).

42   Rounding or Passing Marks and Obstructions

Rule 42 applies when yachts are about to round or pass a *mark*, other than a starting *mark* surrounded by navigable water, on the same required side or an *obstruction* on the same side, except that:

(a) rule 42 shall not apply between two yachts on opposite *tacks* on a beat or when one of them will have to *tack* either to round the *mark* or to avoid the *obstruction*;

(b) rule 42.4 begins to apply when yachts are approaching the starting line to *start*.

42.1   WHEN OVERLAPPED

An Outside Yacht

(a) An outside yacht shall give each inside *overlapping* yacht room to round or pass the *mark* or *obstruction*, except as provided in rule 42.3. Room is the space needed by an inside *overlapping* yacht, which is handled in a seamanlike manner in the prevailing conditions, to pass in safety between an outside yacht and a *mark* or *obstruction*, and includes space to *tack* or *gybe* when either is an integral part of the rounding or passing manoeuvre.

(b) An outside yacht *overlapped* when she comes within two of her overall lengths of a *mark* or *obstruction* shall give room as required, even though the *overlap* may thereafter be broken.

(c) An outside yacht that claims to have broken an *overlap* has the onus of satisfying the race committee that she became *clear ahead* when she was more than two of her overall lengths from the *mark* or *obstruction*.

An Inside Yacht

(d) A yacht that claims an inside *overlap* has the onus of satisfying the race committee that she established the *overlap* in accordance with rule 42.3.

(e) When an inside yacht of two or more *overlapped* yachts, either on opposite *tacks* or on the same *tack* without *luffing* rights, will have to *gybe* in order most directly to assume a *proper course* to the next *mark*, she shall *gybe* at the first reasonable opportunity.

99

42.2 WHEN NOT OVERLAPPED

A Yacht Clear Astern

(a) A yacht *clear astern* when the yacht *clear ahead* comes within two of her overall lengths of a *mark* or *obstruction* shall keep clear in anticipation of and during the rounding or passing manoeuvre, whether the yacht *clear ahead* remains on the same *tack* or *gybes*.

101

(b) A yacht *clear astern* shall not *luff* above *close-hauled* so as to prevent a yacht *clear ahead* from *tacking* to round a *mark*.

102

A Yacht Clear Ahead

(c) A yacht *clear ahead* that *tacks* to round a *mark* is subject to rule 41, (Changing Tacks—Tacking and Gybing).

101

(d) A yacht *clear ahead* shall be under no obligation to give room to a yacht *clear astern* before an *overlap* is established.

102

42.3 EXCEPTIONS AND LIMITATIONS

(a) Limitation on Establishing an Overlap
A yacht that establishes an inside *overlap* from *clear astern* is entitled to room under rule 42.1(a) only when, at that time, the outside yacht:

102
106
103

   (i)   is able to give room, and

   (ii) is more than two of her overall lengths from the *mark* or *obstruction*. However, when a yacht completes a *tack* within two of her overall lengths of a *mark* or *obstruction*, she shall give room as required by rule 42.1(a) to a yacht that cannot thereafter avoid establishing a late inside *overlap*.

104

At a continuing *obstruction*, rule 42.3(b) applies.

(b) Limitation When an Obstruction is a Continuing One.
A yacht *clear astern* may establish an *overlap* between a yacht *clear ahead* and a continuing *obstruction*, such as a shoal or the shore or another vessel, only when, at that time, there is room for her to pass between them in safety.

105
106

(c) Taking an Inside Yacht to the Wrong Side of a Mark.
An outside *leeward yacht* with luffing rights may take an inside yacht to windward of a *mark* provided that she:

105

   (i)   hails to that effect, and

   (ii) begins to *luff* before she is within two of her overall lengths of the *mark*, and

   (iii) also passes to windward of it.

42.4 AT A STARTING MARK SURROUNDED BY NAVIGABLE WATER

When approaching the starting line to *start* and after *starting*, a *leeward yacht* shall be under no obligation to give any *windward yacht* room to pass to leeward of a starting *mark* surrounded by navigable water; but, after the starting signal, a *leeward yacht* shall not deprive a *windward yacht* of room at such a *mark* by sailing either:

107

(a) above the compass bearing of the course to the first *mark,* or

(b) above *close-hauled.*

43 Close-Hauled, Hailing for Room to Tack at Obstructions

43.1 HAILING
When two *close-hauled* yachts are on the same *tack* and safe pilotage requires the yacht *clear ahead* or the *leeward yacht* to make a substantial alteration of course to clear an *obstruction,* and when she intends to *tack,* but cannot *tack* without colliding with the other yacht, she shall hail the other yacht for room to *tack* and clear the other yacht, but she shall not hail and *tack* simultaneously.

43.2 RESPONDING
The hailed yacht at the earliest possible moment after the hail shall:
either

(a) *tack,* in which case the hailing yacht shall begin to *tack,* either:

    (i) before the hailed yacht has completed her *tack,* or

    (ii) when she cannot then *tack* without colliding with the hailed yacht, immediately she is able to *tack* and clear her;

or

(b) reply "You *tack*", or words to that effect, when in her opinion she can keep clear without *tacking* or after postponing her *tack.*
In this case:

    (i) the hailing yacht shall immediately *tack* and

    (ii) the hailed yacht shall keep clear.

    (iii) The onus of satisfying the race committee that she kept clear shall lie on the hailed yacht that replied "You *tack*".

43.3 LIMITATION ON RIGHT TO ROOM TO TACK WHEN THE OBSTRUCTION IS ALSO A MARK

(a) When an *obstruction* is a starting *mark* surrounded by navigable water, or the ground tackle of such a *mark,* and when approaching the starting line to *start* and after *starting,* the yacht *clear ahead* or the *leeward yacht* shall not be entitled to room to *tack.*

(b) At other *obstructions* that are *marks,* when the hailed yacht can fetch the *obstruction,* the hailing yacht shall not be entitled to room to *tack* and clear the hailed yacht, and the hailed yacht shall immediately so inform the hailing yacht. When, thereafter, the hailing yacht again hails for room to *tack* and clear the hailed yacht, the hailed yacht shall, at the earliest possible moment after the hail, give the hailing yacht the required room. After receiving room, the hailing yacht shall either retire immediately or exonerate herself by accepting an alternative penalty when so prescribed in the sailing instructions.

(c) When, after having refused to respond to a hail under rule 43.3(b), the hailed yacht fails to fetch, she shall retire immediately, or exonerate herself by accepting an alternative penalty when so prescribed in the sailing instructions.

44 Returning to Start

44.1 (a) After the starting signal is made, a premature starter returning to *start,* or a yacht working into position from the course side of the starting line or its extensions, shall keep clear of all yachts that are *starting* or have *started* correctly, until she is wholly on the pre-start side of the starting line or its extensions.

(b) Thereafter, she shall be accorded the rights under the rules of Part IV of a yacht that is *starting* correctly; but when she thereby acquires right of way over another yacht that is *starting* correctly, she shall allow that yacht ample room and opportunity to keep clear.

44.2   A premature starter, while continuing to sail the course and until it is obvious that she is returning to *start*, shall be accorded the rights under the rules of Part IV of a yacht that has *started*.

114

45   Re-rounding after Touching a Mark

45.1   A yacht that has touched a *mark*, and is exonerating herself in accordance with rule 52.2, (Touching a Mark), shall keep clear of all other yachts that are about to round or pass it or have rounded or passed it correctly, until she has rounded it completely and has cleared it and is on a *proper course* to the next *mark*.

114
119

45.2   A yacht that has touched a *mark*, while continuing to sail the course and until it is obvious that she is returning to round it completely in accordance with rule 52.2, (Touching a Mark), shall be accorded rights under the rules of Part IV.

46   Person Overboard; Yacht Anchored, Aground or Capsized

46.1   A yacht under way shall keep clear of another yacht *racing* that:

(a) is manoeuvring or hailing for the purpose of rescuing a person overboard, or

(b) is anchored, aground or capsized.

114
115

46.2   A yacht shall not be penalised for fouling a yacht that she is attempting to assist or that goes aground or capsizes immediately in front of her.

46.3   A yacht anchored or aground shall indicate the fact to any yacht that may be in danger of fouling her. Under normal conditions, a hail is sufficient indication. Of two yachts anchored, the one that anchored later shall keep clear, except that a yacht dragging shall keep clear of one that is not.

(Numbers 47, 48 and 49 are spare numbers)

Part V—**Other Sailing Rules**

Obligations of Helmsman and Crew in Handling a Yacht

*A yacht is subject to the rules of Part V only while she is **racing**.*

50   Ranking as a Starter

A yacht whose entry has been accepted and that sails about in the vicinity of the starting line between her preparatory and starting signals shall rank as a starter whether she *starts* or not.

115
116

51   Sailing the Course

51.1   (a) A yacht shall *start* and *finish* only as prescribed in the starting and finishing definitions.

(b) Unless otherwise prescribed in the sailing instructions, a yacht that either crosses prematurely or is on the course side of the starting line or its extensions at the starting signal, shall return and *start* in accordance with the definition.

(c) Unless otherwise prescribed in the sailing instructions, when Code flag "I" has been displayed, and when any part of a yacht's hull, crew or equipment is on the course side of the starting line or its extensions during the minute before her starting signal, she shall return to the pre-start side of the line across one of its extensions and *start*.

(d) Failure of a yacht to see or hear her recall notification shall not relieve her of her obligation to *start* correctly.

116

51.2   A yacht shall sail the course so as to round or pass each *mark* on the required side in correct sequence, and so that a string representing her wake, from the time she *starts* until she *finishes*, would, when drawn taut, lie on the required side of each *mark*, touching each rounding *mark*.

116
117

51.3   A *mark* has a required side for a yacht as long as she is on a leg that it begins, bounds or ends. A starting line *mark* begins to have a required side for a yacht when she *starts*. A starting limit *mark* has a required side for a yacht from the time she is approaching the starting line to *start* until she has left the *mark* astern on the first leg. A finishing line *mark* and a finishing limit *mark* cease to have a required side for a yacht as soon as she *finishes*.

116

51.4   A yacht that rounds or passes a *mark* on the wrong side may exonerate herself by making her course conform to the requirements of rule 51.2.

117

51.5   It is not necessary for a yacht to cross the finishing line completely; after *finishing*, she may clear it in either direction.

118

52   Touching a Mark

52.1   A yacht that either:

(a) touches:

(i)   a starting *mark* before *starting*; or

(ii)   a *mark* that begins, bounds or ends the leg of the course on which she is sailing; or

(iii) a finishing *mark* while *racing*;

or

(b) causes a *mark* or *mark* vessel to shift to avoid being touched,

shall either exonerate herself in accordance with rule 52.2, or act in accordance with rule 68, (Protests by Yachts), when she alleges that she was wrongfully compelled by another yacht to touch it or cause it to shift, unless the other yacht retires or exonerates herself by accepting an alternative penalty when so prescribed in the sailing instructions.

52.2 (a) When a yacht touches a *mark* surrounded by navigable water, she may exonerate herself by completing the rounding of the *mark*, leaving it on the required side and thereafter re-rounding it or re-passing it without touching it, as required to sail the course in accordance with rule 51.2, (Sailing the Course), and the sailing instructions. **119**

(b) When a yacht touches:

(i) a starting *mark*, she shall carry out the rounding after she has *started*; **119**

(ii) a finishing *mark*, she shall carry out the rounding, and she shall not rank as having *finished* until she has completed the rounding and again crosses the finishing line in accordance with the definition of *finishing*.

(c) When a yacht touches a *mark* not surrounded by navigable water, she may exonerate herself by completing one 360° turn at the first reasonable opportunity.

53   Casting Off, Anchoring, Making Fast and Hauling Out   **120**

53.1   AT THE PREPARATORY SIGNAL
A yacht shall be afloat and off moorings at her preparatory signal, but may be anchored.

53.2   WHEN RACING
A yacht may anchor, but shall not make fast or be made fast by means other than anchoring, nor be hauled out, except for the purpose of rule 55, (Aground or Foul of an Obstruction), or to effect repairs, reef sails or bail out.

53.3   MEANS OF ANCHORING
Means of anchoring may include the crew standing on the bottom or any weight lowered to the bottom. A yacht shall recover any anchor or weight used, and any chain or rope attached to it, before continuing in the race, unless, after making every effort, she fails to do so. In this case she shall report the circumstances to the race committee, which may penalise her when it considers the loss due either to inadequate gear or to insufficient effort to recover it.

54   Means of Propulsion

54.1   BASIC RULE

(a) Unless otherwise permitted by this rule, a yacht shall be propelled only by the natural action of the wind on the sails and spars, and the water on the hull and underwater surfaces. A yacht shall not check way by abnormal means. **120**

(b) Sails may be adjusted, and a competitor may move his body in order to maintain or change the angle of heel or fore and aft trim, or to facilitate steering. However, except as provided in rules 54.1(c) and 54.3, no actions, including *tacking* and *gybing*, shall be performed that propel the yacht faster than if the sails, hull and underwater surfaces had been trimmed to best advantage at the time.

(c) A yacht may promote or check way by means other than those permitted by this rule for the purpose of Fundamental Rule A, (Rendering Assistance).

(d) A yacht may anchor as permitted by rules 53, (Casting Off, Anchoring, Making Fast and Hauling Out) and 55, (Aground or Foul or an Obstruction). A yacht shall not recover an anchor in a manner that causes her to pass the point at which the anchor is lifted off the ground.

120

54.2 ACTIONS THAT ARE PROHIBITED
Examples of actions that are prohibited, except as permitted under rules 54.1(b) or 54.3:

(a) Repeated forceful movement of the helm (sculling).

(b) Persistent or rapidly-repeated trimming and releasing of any sail (pumping).

(c) Sudden movement of the body forward or aft (ooching).

(d) Persistent or rapidly-repeated vertical or athwartships body movement.

(e) Movement of the body or adjustment of the sails or centreboard that leads to persistent rolling of the yacht (rocking).

120

54.3 ACTIONS THAT ARE PERMITTED
The following actions are permitted for the sole purpose of accelerating a yacht down the face of a wave (surfing) or, when planing conditions exist, responding to an increase in the velocity of the wind.

(a) Not more than three rapidly-repeated trims and releases of any sail (pumping).

(b) Sudden movement of the body forward or aft (ooching).

There shall be no further pumping or ooching with respect to that wave or increase of wind.

55 Aground or Foul of an Obstruction

A yacht, after grounding or fouling another vessel or other object, is subject to rule 57, (Manual and Stored Power), and may, in getting clear, use her own anchors, boats, ropes, spars and other gear; may send out an anchor in a boat; may be refloated by her crew going overboard either to stand on the bottom or to go ashore to push off; but may receive outside assistance only from the crew of the vessel fouled. A yacht shall recover all her own gear used in getting clear before continuing in the race.

56 Sounding

Any means of sounding may be used, provided that rule 54, (Means of Propulsion), is not infringed.

57 Manual and Stored Power

A yacht shall use manual power only and shall not use any device that derives assistance from stored energy for doing work; except that, when so prescribed in the sailing instructions, a power winch or windlass may be used in weighing anchor or in getting clear after running aground or fouling any object, and a power pump may be used in an auxiliary yacht.

58   **Boarding** | **120**

Unless otherwise prescribed in the sailing instructions, no person shall board a yacht, except for the purposes of Fundamental Rule A, (Rendering Assistance), or to attend an injured or ill member of the crew or temporarily as one of the crew of a vessel fouled.

59   **Leaving, Crew Overboard** |

Unless otherwise prescribed in the sailing instructions, no person on board a yacht when her preparatory signal was made shall leave, unless injured or ill, or for the purposes of Fundamental Rule A, (Rendering Assistance), except that any member of the crew may fall overboard or leave her to swim, stand on the bottom as a means of anchoring, haul her out ashore to effect repairs, reef sails or bail out, or to help her to get clear after grounding or fouling another vessel or object, provided that this person is back on board before the yacht continues in the race.

60   **Outside Assistance**

Except as permitted by Fundamental Rule A, (Rendering Assistance), rule 55, (Aground or Foul of an Obstruction), and rule 58, (Boarding), a yacht shall neither receive outside assistance nor use any gear other than that on board when her preparatory signal was made.

61   **Clothing and Equipment**   **120**

61.1   (a) Except as permitted by rule 61.2, a competitor shall not wear or carry clothing or equipment for the purpose of increasing his weight.

(b) Furthermore, the total weight of clothing and equipment worn or carried by a competitor shall not be capable of exceeding 15 kilograms, when soaked with water and weighed as provided in Appendix 10, (Weighing of Wet Clothing), unless class rules or the sailing instructions prescribe a lesser or greater weight, in which case such weight shall apply, except that it shall not exceed 20 kilograms.

61.2   When so prescribed by the class rules, weight jackets of non-metallic material (excepting normal fasteners), with or without pockets, compartments or containers, shall be permitted, provided that the jacket:

(a) is permanently buoyant,

(b) does not extend more than 30 mm above the competitor's shoulders, and

(c) can be removed by the competitor in less than ten seconds,

and that ballast carried in the pockets, compartments and containers shall only be water. For the purpose of rule 61.1(b), the pockets, compartments and containers shall be filled completely with water and included in the total weight.

61.3   When a competitor is protested or selected for inspection, he shall produce all containers referred to in rule 61.2 that were carried while *racing*.

61.4   The organising authority of an offshore event or events for cruiser-racer type yachts may prescribe that rule 61.1(b) shall not apply to the event or events.

62   **Increasing Stability**   **120**

Unless otherwise prescribed by her class rules or in the sailing instructions, a yacht shall not use any device, such as a trapeze or plank, to project outboard the weight of any of the crew, nor, when lifelines are required by the conditions for the race, shall any member of the crew station any part of his torso outside them, other than temporarily. On yachts equipped with upper and lower lifelines of wire, a crew member sitting on the deck facing outboard with his waist inside the lower lifeline may have the upper part of his body outside the upper lifeline.

63   Skin Friction

A yacht shall not eject or release from a container any substance (such as polymer) the purpose of which is, or could be, to reduce the frictional resistance of the hull by altering the character of the flow of water inside the boundary layer.

64   Setting and Sheeting Sails

64.1   CHANGING SAILS
While changing headsails and spinnakers, a replacing sail may be fully set and trimmed before the sail it replaces is taken in, but only one mainsail and, except when changing, only one spinnaker shall be carried set.

64.2   SHEETING SAILS TO SPARS

(a) Unless otherwise prescribed by the class rules, any sail may be sheeted to or led above a boom regularly used for a working sail and permanently attached to the mast to which the head of the working sail is set, but no sails shall be sheeted over or through outriggers.

(b) An outrigger is any fitting so placed, except as permitted in rule 64.2(a), that it could exert outward pressure on a sheet at a point from which, with the yacht upright, a vertical line would fall outside the hull or deck planking at that point, or outside such other positions as class rules prescribe. For the purpose of this rule: bulwarks, rails and rubbing strakes are not part of the hull or deck planking. A boom of a boomed headsail that requires no adjustment when *tacking* is not an outrigger.

64.3   SPINNAKER: SPINNAKER BOOM
A spinnaker shall not be set without a boom. The tack of a spinnaker when set and drawing shall be in close proximity to the outboard end of a spinnaker boom. Any headsail may be attached to a spinnaker boom, provided that a spinnaker is not set. Only one spinnaker boom shall be used at a time and, when in use, shall be carried only on the side of the foremost mast opposite to the main boom and shall be fixed to the mast. Rule 64.3 shall not apply when shifting a spinnaker boom or sail attached thereto.

64.4   HEADSAIL
Unless otherwise prescribed by the class rules, the following distinction shall apply between spinnakers and headsails. A headsail is a sail in which its mid-girth, measured between the mid-points of the luff and leech, does not exceed 50% of the length of the foot, and in which any other intermediate girth does not exceed a value similarly proportional to its distance from the head of the sail. A sail tacked down abaft the foremost mast is not a headsail.

65   Flags

A national authority may prescribe the flag usage that shall be observed by yachts under its jurisdiction.

66   Fog Signals and Lights

Every yacht shall observe the International Regulations for Preventing Collisions at Sea or Government Rules for fog signals and, as a minimum, the exhibition of lights at night.

(Number 67 is a spare number)

Part VI—**Protests, Penalties and Appeals**

Definitions

When a term defined below is used in its defined sense in Part VI and associated appendices, it is printed in **bold type**. *The definitions rank as rules.*

Rules—

(a) These racing rules, and

(b) the prescriptions of the national authority concerned, when they apply, and

(c) the sailing instructions, and

(d) the appropriate class rules, and

(e) any other conditions governing the event.

Protest—A written allegation by a yacht under rule 68, (Protests by Yachts), that another yacht has infringed a **rule** or **rules**.

The term **protest** includes when appropriate:

(a) a request for redress under rule 69, (Requests for Redress); or

(b) a request for a hearing under rule 70.1, (Action by Race or Protest Committee), or Appendix 3, rule 2.6, (Alternative Penalties); or

(c) a notification of a hearing under rule 70.2, (Action by Race or Protest Committee); or

(d) an investigation of redress under rule 70.3, (Yacht Materially Prejudiced); or

(e) a report by a measurer under rule 70.4, (Measurer's Responsibility).

Party to a Protest—The protesting yacht, the protested yacht, the race committee or any yacht involved in the incident that might be penalised as a result of the **protest**.

Protest Committee—The body appointed to hear and decide **protests** in accordance with rule 1.5, (Authority for Organising, Conducting and Judging Races), namely:

(a) the race committee or a sub-committee thereof; or

(b) a separate and independent protest committee or jury; or

(c) an international jury.

Interested Party—Anyone who stands to gain or lose as a result of a decision of a **protest committee** or who has a close personal interest in the result.

SECTION A—Initiation of Action

68   Protests by Yachts

68.1   RIGHT TO PROTEST
A yacht can protest any other yacht, except that a **protest** for an alleged infringement of the rules of Part IV can be made only by a yacht directly involved in, or witnessing an incident.

68.2   DURING A RACE—PROTEST FLAG   **121**

(a) An intention to protest an infringement of the **rules** occurring during a race shall be signified by the protesting yacht conspicuously displaying a flag. Code flag 'B' is always acceptable, irrespective of any other provisions in the sailing instructions.

(b) The flag shall be displayed at the first reasonable opportunity after the incident.

(c)   (i)   Except as provided in rule 68.2(c)(ii), the flag shall be displayed until the yacht *finishes* or, when the first opportunity occurs after *finishing*, until acknowledged by the race committee.

       (ii)   In the case of a yacht sailed single-handed, it will be sufficient to display the flag at the first reasonable opportunity after the incident and to bring it to the notice of the race committee when the protesting yacht *finishes*.

(d) When the yacht retires, the flag shall be displayed until she has informed the race committee or has left the vicinity of the course.

68.3   AFTER A RACE
A yacht may protest without having displayed a protest flag:

(a) when she has no knowledge of the facts justifying a **protest** until she has *finished* or retired, or

(b) when a yacht, having displayed a protest flag, fails to lodge a valid **protest** as required by rule 33.2, (Contact between Yachts Racing) or rule 52, (Touching a Mark).

68.4   INFORMING THE PROTESTED YACHT   **121**
A protesting yacht shall try to inform the yacht she intends to protest that a **protest** will be lodged. When an alternative penalty is prescribed in the sailing instructions, she shall hail the other yacht immediately.

68.5   PARTICULARS TO BE INCLUDED   **121**
A **protest** shall be in writing and be signed by the owner or his representative, and include the following particulars:

(a) the date, time and whereabouts of the incident;

(b) the particular **rule** or **rules** alleged to have been infringed;

(c) a description of the incident;

(d) unless irrelevant, a diagram of the incident.

68.6   TIME LIMIT
Unless otherwise prescribed in the sailing instructions, a protesting yacht shall deliver or, when that is not possible, mail her **protest** to the race committee:

(a) within two hours of the time she *finishes* the race or within such time as may have been prescribed in the sailing instructions, unless the **protest committee** has reason to extend this time limit, or

(b) when she does not *finish* the race, within such time as the **protest committee** considers reasonable in the circumstances.

68.7   FEE
Unless otherwise prescribed in the sailing instructions, a **protest** shall not be accompanied by a fee.

68.8   REMEDYING DEFECTS IN THE PROTEST
The **protest committee** shall allow the protesting yacht to remedy during the hearing:

(a) any defects in the details required by rule 68.5, provided that the **protest** identifies the nature of the incident, and

(b) a failure to deposit such fee as may be required under rule 68.7.

68.9   WITHDRAWING A PROTEST
When a written **protest** has been lodged, it shall not be withdrawn, but shall be decided by the **protest committee**, unless prior to the hearing one or more of the yachts acknowledges the infringement, except that, when the **protest committee** finds that contact between two yachts was minor and unavoidable, a protesting yacht may withdraw her **protest**.

69   Requests for Redress

A yacht that alleges that her finishing position has been materially prejudiced through no fault of her own by:

(a) an action or omission of the race committee, or

(b) rendering assistance in accordance with Fundamental Rule A, (Rendering Assistance), or

(c) being disabled by another vessel that was required to keep clear, (a yacht is "disabled" when, in the absence of other yachts, she is significantly impaired in her ability to proceed at normal speed or to manoeuvre or to proceed in safety), or

(d) a yacht infringing Fundamental Rule C, (Fair Sailing), or against which a penalty has been imposed under rule 75.1, (Penalties by the Race Committee or Protest Committee),

may request redress from the **protest committee** in accordance with the requirements for a **protest** provided in rules 68.5, 68.6, 68.7 and 68.8, (Protests by Yachts). A protest flag need not be displayed. The **protest committee** shall then proceed in accordance with rule 74.2, (Consideration of Redress).

70   Action by Race or Protest Committee

70.1   WITHOUT A HEARING
The race committee may act in accordance with rule 74.4, (Penalties), without a hearing against a yacht that:

(a) fails either to *start* or *finish*, except that she shall be entitled to a hearing when she satisfies the **protest committee** that an error may have been made, or

(b) when the Percentage Penalty as set out in Appendix 3 is in effect, displays Code flag "I" during a race but fails to report the infringement and is thus subject to Appendix 3, rule 2.6.

A yacht so penalised shall be informed of the action taken, either by letter or by notification in the race results.

70.2   WITH A HEARING
The race committee or the **protest committee** may call a hearing when it:

(a) sees an apparent infringement by a yacht of any of the **rules** (except as provided in rule 70.1), or

(b) learns directly from a written or oral statement by a yacht (including one contained in an invalid **protest**) that she may have infringed a **rule**, or

(c) has reasonable grounds for believing that an infringement resulted in serious damage, or

(d) receives a report not later than the same day from a witness who was neither competing in the race nor otherwise an **interested party**, alleging an infringement, or

(e) has reasonable grounds for supposing, from the evidence at the hearing of a valid **protest**, that any yacht involved in the incident may have committed an infringement.

For such hearings, the race committee or **protest committee** shall notify the yacht involved thereof in writing, delivered or mailed not later than 1800 on the day after:

(i)   the finish of the race, or

(ii)   the receipt of the report, or

(iii)   the hearing of the **protest**.

When rule 70.2(e) applies, this notice may be given orally at the hearing. The notice shall identify the incident, the **rule** or **rules** alleged to have been infringed and the time and place of the hearing.

70.3   YACHT MATERIALLY PREJUDICED
The race committee or the **protest committee** may initiate consideration of redress when it is satisfied that any of the circumstances set out in rule 69, (Requests for Redress), may have occurred.

70.4   MEASURER'S RESPONSIBILITY
When a measurer concludes that a yacht does not comply with her class rules or measurement or rating certificate:

(a) before a race or series; he shall request the owner or his representative to correct the defect. When the defect is not corrected, he shall report the matter in writing, which shall reject or rescind the yacht's entry or approve the entry in accordance with rule 19, (Measurement or Rating Certificates). The yacht shall be entitled to a hearing upon her request.

(b) after a race; he shall make a report to the race committee or to the **protest committee**, which shall then notify the yacht concerned and call a hearing.

The measurer shall not have the authority either to rescind an entry or to disqualify a yacht.

121

SECTION B—**Protest Procedure**

71   Procedural Requirements

71.1   REQUIREMENT FOR A HEARING
A yacht shall not be penalised without a hearing, except as provided in rule 70.1, (Action by Race or Protest Committee).

71.2   INTERESTED PARTIES

(a) No member of a **protest committee** shall take part in the discussion or decision upon any disputed question in which he is an **interested party**, but this does not preclude him from giving evidence in such a case.

(b) A **party to a protest** who wishes to object to a member of the **protest committee** on the grounds that he is an **interested party** shall do so before evidence is taken at the hearing or as soon thereafter as he becomes aware of the conflict of interest.

71.3   PROTESTS BETWEEN YACHTS IN SEPARATE RACES
A **protest** occurring between yachts competing in separate races organised by different clubs shall be heard by a combined committee of the clubs concerned.

72   Acceptance or Refusal of a Protest

72.1   ACCEPTING A PROTEST
When the **protest committee** decides after examination that a **protest** conforms to all the requirements of rule 68, (Protests by Yachts) and is valid, it shall then call a hearing as soon as possible.

72.2   REFUSING A PROTEST
When the **protest committee** decides that a **protest** does not conform to the requirements of rule 68, (Protests by Yachts), all **parties to the protest** concerned shall be notified that the **protest** will not be heard and of the reason for such decision. Such a decision shall not be reached without giving the protesting party an opportunity of bringing evidence that the requirements of rule 68 were met.

72.3   NOTIFICATION OF PARTIES
The **protest**, or a copy of it, shall be made available to all **parties to the protest**, and each shall be notified of the time and place of the hearing. A reasonable time shall be allowed for the preparation of a defence.

73   Hearings

73.1   RIGHT TO BE PRESENT
The **parties to the protest**, or a representative of each, shall have the right to be present throughout the hearing of all the evidence and to question witnesses. Each witness, unless he is a member of the **protest committee**, shall be excluded, except when giving his evidence. Others may be admitted as observers at the discretion of the **protest committee**.

73.2   TAKING OF EVIDENCE
The **protest committee** shall take the evidence presented by the **parties to the protest** and such other evidence as it deems necessary.

73.3   EVIDENCE OF COMMITTEE MEMBER
Any member of the **protest committee** who speaks of his own observation of the incident shall give his evidence as a witness in the presence of the **parties to the protest**, and may be questioned.

73.4   FAILURE TO ATTEND

Failure on the part of any **party to the protest**, or a representative, to make an effort to attend the hearing may justify the **protest committee** in deciding the **protest** as it thinks fit without a full hearing.

73.5   RE-OPENING A HEARING

A hearing may be re-opened when the **protest committee** decides it may have made a significant error or when material new evidence becomes available within a reasonable time. Requests from yachts for re-opening a hearing shall be lodged no later than 1800 of the day following the decision, unless the **protest committee** has reason to extend this time limit.

74   Decisions and Penalties

74.1   FINDING OF FACTS

The **protest committee** shall determine the facts and base its decision upon them. The finding of facts shall not be subject to appeal.

74.2   CONSIDERATION OF REDRESS

(a) When consideration of redress has been initiated as provided in rule 69, (Requests for Redress), or rule 70.3, (Yacht Materially Prejudiced), the **protest committee** shall decide whether the finishing position of a yacht or yachts has been materially prejudiced in any of the circumstances set out in rule 69.

(b) If so, the **protest committee** shall satisfy itself by taking appropriate evidence, especially before *abandoning* or *cancelling* the race, that it is aware of the relevant facts and of the probable consequences of any arrangement, to all yachts concerned for that particular race and for the series, if any, as a whole.

(c) The **protest committee** shall then make as equitable an arrangement as possible for all yachts concerned. This may be to let the results of the race stand, to adjust the points score or the finishing time of the prejudiced yacht, to *abandon* or *cancel* the race or to adopt some other means.

74.3   MEASUREMENT PROTESTS

(a) A **protest** under rule 19, (Measurement or Rating Certificates), or class rules that a measurement, scantling or flotation rule has been infringed while *racing*, or that a classification or rating certificate is invalid, may be decided by the **protest committee** immediately after the hearing, provided that it is satisfied there is no reasonable doubt as to the interpretation or application of the rules. When the **protest committee** is not so satisfied, it shall refer the question, together with the facts found, to an authority qualified to resolve such questions. The **protest committee**, in making its decision, shall be governed by the report of the authority.

(b) In addition to the requirements of rule 74.7, the body that issued the certificate of the yacht concerned shall also be notified.

(c) When an appeal under rule 77, (Appeals), is lodged, the yacht may compete in further races, but subject to the results of that appeal.

74.4   PENALTIES

When the **protest committee** after finding the facts, or the race committee acting under rule 70.1, (Action by Race or Protest Committee), decides that:

(a) a yacht has infringed any of the **rules**, or

(b) in consequence of her neglect of any of the **rules**, a yacht has compelled other yachts to infringe any of the **rules**,

she shall be disqualified, unless the sailing instructions applicable to that race provide some other penalty and, in the case of (b), the other yachts shall be exonerated. Such disqualification or other penalty shall be imposed irrespective of whether the **rule** that led to the disqualification or penalty was mentioned in the **protest**, or the yacht that was at fault was mentioned or protested, e.g., the protesting yacht or a third yacht may be disqualified and the protested yacht exonerated.

74.5   ALTERNATIVE PENALTIES
When so prescribed in the sailing instructions, the procedure and penalty for infringing a rule of Part IV shall be as provided in Appendix 3, Alternative Penalties for Infringement of a Rule of Part IV.

74.6   POINTS AND PLACES
(a) For the purpose of awarding points in a series, a retirement after an infringement of the **rules** shall not rank as a disqualification. This penalty can be imposed only in accordance with rule 74.4.

(b) When a yacht either is disqualified or has retired, the following yachts shall each be moved up one place.

(c) When a yacht is penalised by being removed from a series or a part of a series, no races are to be rescored and no changes are to be made in the scores of other yachts, except that, when the incident from which the penalty resulted occurred in a particular race, she shall be disqualified from that race and yachts *finishing* behind her in that race shall each be moved up one place.

74.7   THE DECISION
(a) After making its decision, the **protest committee** shall promptly communicate the following to the **parties to the protest**:

(i)   the facts found,

(ii)   the **rule** or **rules** judged applicable,

(iii)   the decision and grounds on which it is based,

(iv)   the yacht or yachts penalised, if any, and

(v)   the penalty imposed, if any, or the redress granted, if any.

(b) A **party to the protest** shall on request be supplied with:

(i)   the above details in writing, and

(ii)   unless irrelevant, a diagram of the incident endorsed by the **protest committee**.

SECTION C—**Special Rules**

75   Gross Infringement of Rules or Misconduct

75.1   PENALTIES BY THE RACE COMMITTEE OR PROTEST COMMITTEE
After a finding of gross infringement of the **rules** or of a gross breach of good manners or sportsmanship, the race committee or **protest committee**

may exclude a competitor, and a yacht when appropriate, either from further participation in a series or from the whole series, or take other disciplinary action, proceeding in accordance with rules 73, (Hearings), and 74.1, (Finding of Facts). The committee shall report any penalty imposed to the national authority and to the national authority of the competitor and of the yacht.

75.2   PENALTIES BY THE NATIONAL AUTHORITY
Upon receipt of a report of gross infringement of the **rules** or a gross breach of good manners or sportsmanship or a report of a penalty imposed under rule 75.1, a national authority may conduct an investigation and, when appropriate, a hearing and take such action as it deems appropriate against the person or persons or the yacht involved. Such action may include disqualification from participating in any race held in its jurisdiction for any period or other disciplinary action. The national authority shall report any penalty imposed to the national authority of the competitor and of the yacht and to the International Yacht Racing Union. The IYRU shall inform all national authorities, which may also apply a penalty.

76   **Liability**

76.1   DAMAGES
The question of damages arising from an infringement of any of the **rules** shall be governed by the prescriptions, if any, of the national authority.

76.2   MEASUREMENT EXPENSES
Unless otherwise prescribed by the **protest committee**, the fees and expenses entailed by a **protest** on measurement or classification shall be paid by the unsuccessful party.

SECTION D—Appeal Procedure

77   **Appeals**

77.1   RIGHT OF APPEAL
Except when governed by rule 1.7 (Authority for Organising, Conducting and Judging Races), the following appeals and references may be made to the national authority concerned:

    (a) a yacht that is a **party to a protest** may appeal against a decision of a **protest committee**;

    (b) a race committee may appeal only against a decision of an independent protest committee constituted as provided in rule 1.5(c), (Authority for Organising, Conducting and Judging Races);

    (c) a race committee or protest committee may refer its own decision for confirmation or correction of its interpretation of the **rules**;

    (d) a person or a yacht penalised under rule 75.1, (Penalties by the Race Committee or Protest Committee), may appeal against the decision.

77.2   TIME LIMIT AND DEPOSIT
An appeal or reference shall be made within such period after receipt of the **protest committee's** decision and be accompanied by such deposit as the national authority may prescribe.

77.3   INTERPRETATION OF RULES
An appeal or reference shall be made solely on a question of interpretation of the **rules**. A national authority shall accept the **protest committee's**

121

finding of facts, except that, when it is not satisfied with the facts presented, it may, when practicable, request further information or return the case to the **protest committee** for a re-hearing.

77.4 WITHDRAWAL OF APPEAL
An appeal lodged with the national authority may be withdrawn when the appellant accepts the original decision.

77.5 INTERESTED PARTIES
No **interested party** nor any member of the **protest committee** concerned shall take part in the discussion or the decision upon an appeal or reference.

77.6 POWER TO UPHOLD OR REVERSE A DECISION
The national authority shall have the power to uphold or reverse a decision, and when it is of the opinion, from the facts found by the **protest committee**, that any yacht that is a **party to the protest** has infringed an applicable **rule**, it shall disqualify or penalise her, irrespective of whether the **rule** that led to the disqualification was mentioned in the decision.

77.7 DECISIONS
The decision of the national authority shall be final and shall be communicated in writing to all the **parties to the protest**, who shall be bound by the decision.

78 Particulars to be Supplied in Appeals

78.1 The appeal or reference to the national authority shall be in writing and shall contain the following particulars, so far as they are applicable:

(a) a copy of the notice of race or regatta, the sailing instructions and amendments thereto, and any other conditions governing the event;

(b) a copy of the **protest** or **protests** prepared in accordance with rule 68.5, (Protests by Yachts), and of all other written statements that may have been submitted by the **parties to the protest**;

(c) the observations of the **protest committee** thereon, a full statement of the facts found, the decision and the grounds thereof;

(d) a diagram, prepared or endorsed by the **protest committee** in accordance with the facts found by it, showing:

(i) the course to the next *mark*, or, when close by, the *mark* itself with the required side;

(ii) the direction and force of the wind;

(iii) the set and rate of the tidal stream or current, if any;

(iv) the depth of the water, if relevant, and

(v) the positions and tracks of all yachts involved. It is preferable to show yachts sailing from the bottom of the diagram towards the top;

(e) the grounds of the appeal to be supplied by the appellant in accordance with rule 77.3, (Appeals);

(f) the observations, if any, upon the appeal by the **protest committee**, the race committee or any of the **parties to the protest**.

78.2 The race committee shall notify all **parties to the protest** that an appeal will be lodged and shall invite them to make observations upon it. Any such observations shall be forwarded with the appeal.

APPENDIX 1—Definition of an Amateur and Eligibility Regulations

1   Amateur

1.1   For the purpose of international yacht races in which yachts are required to have one or more amateurs on board and in other races with similar requirements, an amateur is a yachtsman who engages in yacht racing as a pastime as distinguished from a means of obtaining a livelihood or part-time compensation. No yachtsman shall lose amateur status by reason of his livelihood being derived from designing or constructing yachts, yacht parts, sails or accessories; or from similar professions associated with the sport; or solely from the maintenance (but not the *racing*) of yachts.

1.2   Competing in a race or series in which a monetary prize is offered, or a prize having a value greater than US$300, other than a prize awarded only for temporary possession, is ground for loss of amateur status unless prior to the event:

    (i)   the competitor assigns to the IYRU, his national authority or his national Olympic committee all his rights to such prize, or

    (ii)   the organising authority obtains its national authority's consent to a prize (not being money) having a value greater than US$300.

1.3   Any yachtsman whose amateur status is questioned or is in doubt may apply to his national authority for recognition of his amateur status. Any such applicant may be required to provide such particulars and evidence and to pay such fees as the national authority may prescribe. Recognition may be suspended or cancelled by the national authority granting it, and, upon application by the competitor affected, the authority may reinstate recognition of amateur status following a period of at least two years absence from the sport.

1.4   The Permanent Committee of the IYRU or any tribunal nominated by the chairman of that committee may review the decision of any national authority affecting the amateur status of a yachtsman for the purpose of competing in international races.

1.5   For the purpose of participation in the Olympic Regatta an amateur is required to conform to the eligibility rules of the International Olympic Committee. Information on these eligibility requirements is available from all national authorities.

2   I.O.C. Rule 26—Eligibility Code

To be eligible for participation in the Olympic Games, a competitor must:

    —   observe and abide by the Rules of the International Olympic Committee (IOC) and in addition the rules of his or her International Federation (IF), as approved by the IOC, even if the Federation's rules are more strict than those of the IOC;

    —   not have received any financial rewards or material benefit in connection with his or her sports participation, except as permitted in the bye-laws to this rule.

BYE-LAWS TO RULE 26

A.   Each IF is responsible for the wording of the eligibility code relating to its sport, which must be approved by the Executive Board in the name of the IOC.

B.   The observation of Rule 26 and of the eligibility codes of IFs are under the responsibility of IFs and National Olympic Committee (NOC) involved. The Eligibility Commission of the IOC will ensure the application of these provisions.

C.   All cases of infringement of Rule 26 of the IOC and of the eligibility codes of IFs shall be communicated by the respective IF or NOC to the IOC to be taken in consideration by its eligibility commission. In accordance with Rule 23 and its bye-law, the accused competitor may request to be heard by the Executive Board whose decision will be final.

GUIDELINES TO ELIGIBILITY CODE FOR THE IFs

A.   The following regulations are based on the principle that an athlete's health must not suffer nor must he or she be placed at a social or material disadvantage as a result of his or her preparation for and participation in the Olympic Games and international sports competitions. In accordance with Rule 26, the IOC, the IFs, the NOCs, and the National Authorities will assume responsibility for the protection and support of athletes.

B.   All competitors, men or women, who conform to the criteria set out in Rule 26, may participate in the Olympic Games, except those who have:

1.   been registered as professional athletes or professional coaches in any sport. Each National Authority shall provide a means for registering professional yachtsmen and women, and professional coaches. In this connection:

   (a)   Professional yachtsmen or women shall be persons who do not comply with the definition of an amateur as defined in Appendix 1 of the current Yacht Racing Rules.

   (b)   Professional coaches shall be persons who obtain their principal means of livelihood from teaching the skills of yacht racing.

2.   signed a contract as a professional athlete or professional coach in any sport before the official closing of the Olympic Games.

3.   accepted without the knowledge of their IF, National Authority or NOC a material advantage for their preparation or participation in yachting competition except:

   (a)   either from, or with the permission of their National Authority; or

   (b)   from funds held by the National Authority however obtained which are being held by that Authority or Trust for or on behalf of either an individual or class of yachtsmen.

   (c)   National Authorities may issue guidelines for the receipt of such material advantages which shall cover:

      (i)   Reimbursement of expenses properly incurred in preparation for, and competing in an international or Olympic event.

      (ii)   The provision of equipment for such events.

(iii) Living and accommodation allowances and including allowances in lieu of normal salary, etc., if the same is lost due to the yachtsman engaging in such preparation or competition.

(d) The receipt of money as a prize, or otherwise, not exceeding US$300 shall not be a breach of this clause.

4. allowed their person, name, picture, or sports performances to be used for advertising, except when their IF, NOC or National Authority has entered into a contract for sponsorship or equipment. All payment must be made to the IF, NOC or National Authority concerned, and not to the athlete.

5. carried advertising material on their person or clothing in the Olympic Games and Games under the patronage of the IOC, other than trademarks on technical equipment or clothing as agreed by the IOC with the IFs.

In the absence of any special agreement by the IOC with the IF's, advertising material on clothing shall not exceed that on clothing commercially available to the public *provided however* that only one maker's mark may be displayed on clothing worn by yachtsmen and provided that such a mark shall fit within a square not exceeding 100mm by 100mm.

6. in the practice of sport and in the opinion of the IOC, manifestly contravened the spirit of fair play in the exercise of sport, particularly by the use of doping or violence.

APPENDIX 2—Sailboard Racing Rules

A sailboard is a yacht using a free sail system. A free sail system means a swivel-mounted mast not supported in a permanent position while sailing. Sailboard races shall be sailed under the International Yacht Racing Rules modified as follows:

1   Part I—Definitions

1.1   *Leeward* and *Windward*—The *windward* side of a sailboard is the side that is, or, when head to wind or with the wind astern, was, towards the wind, regardless of the direction in which the sailboard is sailing, except when the wind is coming over her stern from the same side as her sail and boom are on, in which case the *windward* side is the other side. The opposite side is the *leeward* side.

When neither of two sailboards on the same *tack* is *clear astern*, the one on the *windward* side of the other is the *windward sailboard*. The other is the *leeward sailboard*.

1.2   *Capsized* and *Recovering*

(a) *Capsized*—A sailboard shall rank as being *capsized* from the moment her masthead touches the water until her masthead is lifted from the water.

(b) *Recovering*—A sailboard shall rank as *recovering* from a capsize from the moment her masthead is lifted from the water until her sail is out of the water and has filled.

2   Part III—General Requirements

2.1   Rule 19—Measurement or Rating Certificates

Rule 19.1—When so prescribed by the national authority, a numbered and dated device on the board, daggerboard and sail shall rank as a measurement certificate.

2.2   Rule 23—Anchor

An anchor and chain or rope need not be carried.

2.3   Rule 24—Life Saving Equipment

A safety line shall prevent the mast separating from the hull.

2.4   Rule 25—Class Insignia, National Letters and Sail Numbers

Rule 25.1(a)—The class insignia shall be displayed once on each side of the sail. It shall fit within a rectangle of 0.5 m², the longer dimension of which shall not exceed one metre. It shall not refer to anything other than the manufacturer or class and shall not consist of more than two letters and three numbers. When approved by the IYRU or a national authority within its jurisdiction, this insignia shall not be considered to be advertising.

Rule 25.1(c)—A sailboard shall carry on her sail a sail number allotted either to the board or to its owner. This number shall be issued by a national authority or its duly authorised body.

3   Part IV—Right of Way Rules

3.1   Rule 33.2—Contact between Yachts Racing

As between each other, rule 33.2 shall not apply to sailboards.

3.2   Rule 38.2—Same Tack—Luffing and Sailing above a Proper Course after Starting

Rule 40—Same Tack—Luffing before Starting

For "mainmast" read "foot of mast".

3.3   Recovering from a Capsize

A sailboard *recovering* from a *capsize* shall not obstruct a sailboard or yacht under way.

3.4   Sail out of the Water when Starting

When approaching the starting line to *start*, a sailboard shall have her sail out of the water and in a normal position, except when *capsized* unintentionally.

3.5   Sailing Backward when Starting

When approaching the starting line to *start* or when on the course side of the starting line, a sailboard sailing or drifting backward shall keep clear of other sailboards or yachts that are *starting* or have *started* correctly.

4   Part V—Other Sailing Rules

Rule 54.1—Means of Propulsion

Dragging a foot in the water to check way is permissible.

5 **Part VI—Protests, Penalties and Appeals**

Rule 68—Protests by Yachts

A sailboard need not display a flag in order to signify her intention to protest as required by rule 68.2, but, except when rule 68.3 applies, she shall notify the other sailboard or yacht by hail at the first reasonable opportunity and the race committee as soon as possible after *finishing* or retiring.

6 **APPENDIX 3—Alternative Penalties for Infringement of a Rule of Part IV**

6.1 720° Turns

Two full 360° turns of the board shall satisfy the provision of the 720° turns penalty. The sailing instructions may prescribe a greater penalty by increasing the number of turns required.

6.2 Percentage

A sailboard need not display Code flag "I" to acknowledge an infringement. She shall notify the other sailboard or yacht by hail immediately and the race committee as soon as possible after *finishing* or retiring.

7 **Rules for Multi-Mast Sailboards**

7.1 Part IV—Rule 38.2 and Rule 40

The normal station of the helmsman is the normal station of the crew member controlling the mainsail. The mainsail is the foremost sail and the mainmast is the foremost mast.

7.2 Appendix 2—Rule 1.2(a) *Capsized*

A multi-mast sailboard shall rank as being *capsized* from the moment all her mastheads touch the water until one masthead is lifted from the water.

7.3 Appendix 2—Rule 1.2(b) *Recovering*

A multi-mast sailboard shall rank as a sailboard *recovering* from a *capsize* from the moment one masthead is lifted from the water until all her sails are out of the water and they have filled.

7.4 Appendix 2—Rule 3.4—Sail out of the Water when Starting

For "sail" read "sails".

APPENDIX 3—Alternative Penalties for Infringement of a Rule of Part IV

Experience indicates that the 720° turns penalty is most satisfactory for small boats in relatively short races, but that it can be dangerous for large yachts and in restricted waters and not sufficiently severe in long races. The 20% penalty is relatively mild and is designed to encourage acknowledgement of infringements and willingness to protest when not acknowledged. Both systems keep yachts racing.

Either of the following alternatives to disqualification may be used by including in the sailing instructions a provision such as the following (or if preferred the selected penalty may be quoted in full):

"The 720° turns penalty (or the percentage penalty) as provided in rule 74.5, (Alternative Penalties), and Appendix 3, Alternative Penalties for Infringement of a

Rule of Part IV, of the yacht racing rules shall apply for infringement of a rule of Part IV."

1   720° Turns

A yacht that acknowledges infringing a rule of Part IV may exonerate herself by making two full 360° turns (720°), subject to the following provisions:

1.1   When the yacht infringed against intends to protest, she shall act in accordance with rule 68, (Protests by Yachts), and hail the infringing yacht immediately.

1.2   With or without such notification, a yacht that realises that she has infringed a rule of Part IV shall acknowledge her infringement by immediately starting to get clear of other yachts and, when well clear, shall forthwith make her turns. While doing so, she shall keep clear of all other yachts until she has completed her turns and is on a *proper course* for the next *mark*.

1.3   The turns may be made in either direction but both in the same direction, with the second full 360° turn following immediately on the first.

1.4   When the infringement occurs before the starting signal, the infringing yacht shall make her turns after the starting signal.

1.5   When an infringement occurs at the finishing line, the infringing yacht shall make her turns on the last leg of the course before being officially *finished*.

1.6   When a yacht acknowledges fault but claims that the other yacht involved in the incident has infringed a rule of Part IV, she shall act in accordance with rule 68, (Protests by Yachts), hail the other yacht immediately and exonerate herself by making her turns. She shall not be further penalised for the infringement she has acknowledged by making her turns, except as set out in paragraphs 1.9 and 1.10.

1.7   When neither yacht acknowledges fault, a **protest** may be lodged in accordance with rule 68, (Protests by Yachts), and the sailing instructions.

1.8   Failure to observe the above requirements will render a yacht that has infringed a rule of part IV liable to disqualification or other penalty, but when an infringing yacht's turns do not conform to the above requirements, the yacht infringed against is relieved of further obligations under rule 33.2, (Contact between Yachts Racing).

1.9   An infringing yacht involved in a collision that results in serious damage to either yacht shall be liable to disqualification.

1.10   The **protest committee** may disqualify a yacht for an infringement of the rules that results in an advantage to the infringing yacht after completing the 720° turns, whether or not serious damage results. The **protest committee's** action shall be governed by rule 70.2, (Action by Race or Protest Committee).

2   Percentage

2.1   A yacht that acknowledges infringing a rule of Part IV shall receive a score for the place worse than her actual finishing position by 20% of the number of starters but not less than three places, subject to the limitation in paragraph 2.8. A yacht infringing a rule in more than one incident shall receive a penalty for each infringement.

2.2 The **protest committee** may disqualify a yacht for serious infringement of the rules, whether or not serious damage resulted.

2.3 When a yacht infringed against intends to **protest**, she shall hail the infringing yacht immediately and act in accordance with rule 68, (Protests by Yachts).

2.4 A yacht that acknowledges infringing a rule of Part IV shall, at the first reasonable opportunity, display Code flag "I" and keep it displayed until she has *finished*. She shall report ackowledging her infringement and identify the yacht infringed against to the race committee within the time limit for lodging protests.

2.5 A yacht that fails to acknowledge an infringement fully as provided in paragraph 2.4 and that, after a **protest** and hearing, is found to have infringed a rule of Part IV, shall be disqualified. However, a yacht that *finishes* and subsequently acknowledges an infringement of a rule of Part IV prior to a hearing shall be penalised 50% or at least six places.

2.6 A yacht that has displayed Code flag "I" during a race and has not reported the infringement to the race committee shall be liable to the 50% penalty of paragraph 2.5 without a hearing except that she may request a hearing on the two points of having displayed the flag and having reported the infringement to the race committee.

2.7 When a yacht has failed to fully acknowledge infringing a rule of Part IV, but the yacht infringed against has not met the requirements of paragraph 2.3, the penalty shall be 20%.

2.8 The penalty shall be computed as 20% (or 50%) of the number of starters in the event to the nearest whole number (round .5 upward), such number to be not less than three (or six), except that a yacht shall not receive a score worse than for one position more than the number of starters. (Examples: an infringing yacht finishing 8th in a start for 19 yachts would receive a score for 12th place: $8 + (19 \times 20\% = 3.8$ or $4) = 12$. Another infringing yacht, finishing 18th, would receive the score for 20th place.) The imposition of a percentage penalty shall not affect the scores of other yachts. Thus, two yachts may receive the same score.

APPENDIX 4—Team Racing Rules

Team racing shall be sailed under the International Yacht Racing Rules supplemented as follows:

1 Sailing Rules

1.1 A yacht may manoeuvre against a yacht sailing on another leg of the course only when she can do so while sailing a *proper course* relative to the leg on which she herself is sailing. For the purpose of this rule, each time a leg is sailed, it shall be regarded as "another leg of the course".

1.2 Except to protect her own or a team mate's finishing position, a yacht in one team that is completing the last leg of the course shall not manoeuvre against a yacht in another team that has no opponent astern of her.

1.3 Right of way may be waived by team mates, provided that in so doing, rule 35, (Limitations on Altering Course), is not infringed with respect to an opponent; but when contact occurs between team mates and neither retires immediately, the lower-scoring team mate shall automatically be disqualified or otherwise penalised. This rule overrides rule 33.2, (Contact between Yachts Racing). The benefits of rule 69, (Requests for Redress), shall not be available to a yacht disabled by contact between team mates.

1.4 When two *overlapping* yachts on the same *tack* are in the act of rounding or passing on the required side of a *mark* at which their *proper course* changes:

(a) When the *leeward yacht* is inside, and has *luffing* rights, she may hold her course or *luff*. When she does not have *luffing* rights, she shall promptly assume her *proper course* to the next *mark*, whether or not she has to *gybe*:

(b) When the *windward yacht* is inside, she shall promptly *luff* up to her *proper course* to the next *mark*, or when she cannot assume such *proper course* without *tacking* and does not choose to *tack*, she shall promptly *luff* up to *close-hauled*. This clause does not restrict a *leeward yacht's* right to *luff* under rule 38, (Same Tack—Luffing and Sailing above a Proper Course after Starting).

2 Scoring Each Race

2.1 Yachts shall score three-quarters of a point for first place, two points for second place, three points for third place, and so on.

2.2 A yacht that does not *start*, (including a premature starter that does not respond to a recall), shall score points equal to the number of yachts entitled to *start* in the race.

2.3 A yacht that infringes any rule and retires with reasonable promptness shall score one point more than the number of yachts entitled to *start* in the race, but when her retirement is tardy, or when she fails to retire and is subsequently disqualified, she shall score four points more than the number of yachts entitled to *start* in the race.

2.4 A yacht that infringes a rule shortly before or when *finishing* shall be considered to have retired with reasonable promptness when she notifies the race committee of her retirement as soon as is reasonably practicable.

2.5 A yacht that does not *finish* for a reason other than an infringement shall score points equal to the number of yachts entitled to *start* in the race, except as provided in rule 2.6.

2.6 After all the yachts of one team have *finished* or retired, the race committee may stop the race and award to each yacht of the other team that is still *racing* and under way, the points she would have received had she *finished*.

2.7 The team with the lowest total point score shall be the winner of the race.

3 Reports

3.1 A yacht that retires shall promptly report that fact and the reason therefore to the race committee. When it resulted from a rule infringement, she shall state:

(a) when the infringement occurred;

(b) which yacht(s), if any, was involved in the infringement; and

(c) when she retired.

The sailing instructions may require her to submit within a prescribed time a signed statement covering a, b and c.

3.2   A yacht that fails to report her retirement in accordance with rule 3.1 shall be awarded points on the assumption that she retired tardily owing to a rule infringement.

4   Determining the Winner

4.1   THE WINNER

(a) When two teams only are competing:
The winner shall be the team winning the greater number of races.

(b) When more than two teams are competing in a series consisting of races, each of which is between two teams, the winner shall be the team winning the greatest number of races.

(c) When more than two teams are all competing in each race, the winner shall be the team with lowest total point score in all races.

4.2   BREAKING TIES

(a) A tie shall, when practicable, be broken by a sail-off. The time of the sail-off, if any, shall be set out in the notice of the race or regatta and the sailing instructions.
When a sail-off is impracticable, the tie shall stand, unless progress into a further round requires it to be broken.

(b) When progress into a further round is necessary, the breaking of ties shall be:

(i)   When two teams only are competing:

1 The winner shall be the team with the lower total point score.

2 When the tie remains, it shall be broken in favour of the winner of the last race.

(ii)   When more than two teams are competing in a series consisting of races, each of which is between two teams:

1 When there is a tie between two teams:
The winner shall be the team that won when the two tied teams met.

2 When there is a tie between more than two teams:
(a) The winner shall be the team with the lowest total point score for the races in which the tied teams met each other.
(b) When a tie remains between two of the teams it shall be broken in accordance with subsection 4.2(b)(ii) 1 of this rule.

(iii)   When more than two teams are all competing in each race:

The winner shall be the team that has beaten the other tied team or teams in most races, or when still tied, the team that beat the other tied team or teams in the last race.

Addendum to Team Racing Rules

Rules recommended to apply when the Home Team provides all racing yachts

5 Allotment of Yachts

The home team shall provide the visiting team with a list of the yachts to be used and of the sail numbers allotted to each yacht for the match. The home team shall divide these yachts into as many equal groups as there are competing teams and these groups shall be drawn for by lot for the first race. The yachts shall then be allotted to the crews by each team, except that a helmsman shall not at any time steer the yacht of which he is normally the helmsman. The groups of yachts shall be exchanged between races so that, as far as possible, each group will be sailed in turn by each team. In a two team match after an even number of races, if either team requests that the yachts be regrouped, the home team shall re-divide them into new groups that shall be drawn for by lot; except that for the final odd race of a two-team match, the visiting team may select the group it wishes to sail.

6 Allotment of Sails

When sails as well as yachts are provided by the home team, the sails used by each yacht in the first race shall be used by her throughout the series. The substitution of a spare or extra sail shall not be permitted, unless, because of damage or for some other valid reason, a change is approved by the race committee after notification to all teams.

7 Group Identification

One group shall carry no markings. The second group shall carry dark coloured strips or pennants, and additional groups shall carry light or differently coloured strips or pennants. Strips or pennants should usually be provided by the home team and should be attached to the same conspicuous place on each yacht of a group, such as the after end of the main boom or the permanent backstay.

8 Breakdowns

8.1 When a breakdown results in material prejudice, the race committee shall decide whether or not it was the fault of the crew. In general, a breakdown caused by defective equipment, or the result of an infringement by an opponent, shall not be deemed the fault of the crew, and a breakdown caused by careless handling or capsizing shall be. In case of doubt, the doubt shall be resolved in favour of the crew.

8.2 When the race committee decides that the breakdown was not the fault of the crew and that a reasonably competent crew could not have remedied the defect in time to prevent material prejudice, it shall award the broken-down yacht the number of points she would have received had she finished in the same position in the race she held when she broke down, or order the race to be resailed, or *cancel* the race. In case of doubt as to her position when she broke down, the doubt shall be resolved against her.

9 Spares

The home team shall be prepared to provide one or more extra yachts and sails to replace any that, in the opinion of the race committee, are unfit for use in the remaining races.

APPENDIX 5—Olympic Scoring System

1   Races to Count

There shall be seven races for each class, of which the best six for each yacht shall be counted for her total points. When it is possible to complete only six races, the best five shall be counted. When it is possible to complete only five races, the best four shall be counted. A minimum of five races is necessary to constitute a series.

2   Scoring

2.1   Each yacht *finishing* in a race and not thereafter retiring or being disqualified shall score points as follows:

Finishing Place	Points
First	0
Second	3
Third	5.7
Fourth	8
Fifth	10
Sixth	11.7
Seventh and thereafter	Place plus 6

Lowest total score wins.

2.2   All other yachts, including a yacht that *finishes* and thereafter retires or is disqualified, shall score points for the finishing place one more than the number of yachts whose entry for the series has been accepted.

3   Redress

In applying rule 69, (Requests for Redress), or rule 70.3, (Yacht Materially Prejudiced), when it is deemed equitable to adjust the score of the prejudiced yacht by awarding points different from those she received for the race in question, the following possibilities may be considered:

(i)   Points equal to the average, to the nearest tenth of a point, of her points in all the races in the series except her worst race and the race in question.

(ii)   Points equal to the average, to the nearest tenth of a point, of the points she had received before the race in question.

(iii)   An arbitrary number of points based on the position of the yacht in the race in question at the time she was prejudiced.

4   Ties

When there is a tie on total points between two or more yachts, the tie shall be broken in favour of the yacht or yachts with the most first places, and when the tie remains the most second places and so on, if necessary, for such races as count for total points. When the tie still remains, it shall stand as part of the final series results.

Note   The following abbreviations are recommended to record the eventualities under paragraphs 2.2 and 3 of the Olympic Scoring System:

DNC   (Did not compete, i.e. did not *start* or rank as a starter under rule 50, (Ranking as a Starter))

DNS   (Did not start, i.e. ranked as a starter under rule 50 but failed to *start*)

PMS	(Started prematurely or otherwise failed to comply with the starting procedure)
RET	(Retired)
DNF	(Did not finish)
DSQ	(Disqualified)
YMP	(Yacht Materially Prejudiced)

Suggested Modifications to the Olympic Scoring System for Use in Certain Series

In a regatta, the difference between the number of entrants and the number of starters is usually insignificant. However, in longer series there may be a large number of entrants who race infrequently, in which case it is recommended that paragraph 2.2 be deleted and that either of the following alternatives be used:

Alternative A

2.2   A yacht that does not *start* or rank as a starter in accordance with rule 50, (Ranking as a Starter), shall score points for the finishing place equal to the number of competitors. A competitor is an entrant who *starts* or ranks as a starter in accordance with rule 50 in any race of the series.

2.3   All other yachts, including a yacht that *finishes* but thereafter retires or is disqualified, shall score points for the finishing place one more than the number of yachts that *started* or ranked as starters in accordance with rule 50 in that race.

Or to avoid rescoring non-starters:

Alternative B

2.2   A yacht that does not *start* or rank as a starter in accordance with rule 50, (Ranking as a Starter), shall score "x" points ("x" to equal points for the finishing place equal to or in excess of the largest number of possible or expected entries in the series).

2.3   All other yachts, including a yacht that *finishes* but thereafter retires or is disqualified, shall score points for the finishing place one more than the number of yachts that *started* or ranked as starters in accordance with rule 50 in that race.

APPENDIX 6—Protest Committee Procedure

Duties of the Protest Committee

In a protest hearing, the **protest committee** should give equal weight to the testimony of all principals; should recognize that honest testimony can vary and even be in conflict as a result of different observations and recollections; should resolve such differences as best it can; should recognize that no yacht is guilty until her infringement has been established to the satisfaction of the **protest committee**; should keep an open mind until all the evidence has been submitted as to whether the protestor or the protestee or a third yacht, when one is involved in the incident, has infringed a **rule**.

1   Preliminaries

1.1   Note on the **protest** the time at which it is received.

1.2 Determine whether the **protest** contains the information called for by rule 68.5, (Protests by Yachts), in sufficient detail to identify the incident and to tell the recipient what the **protest** is about. If not, ask the protestor to supply the information (rule 68.8). When a **protest** by a yacht does not identify the nature of the incident, it shall be refused (rule 68.8(a) and 72.2, (Refusing a Protest)).

1.3 Unless the **protest** already provides the information;

Inquire whether the protestor displayed a protest flag in accordance with rule 68.2, unless rule 68.3 applies or the protestor is seeking redress under rule 69, and note his answer on the **protest**. When a protest flag has not been displayed, the **protest** shall be refused; rule 72, (Acceptance or Refusal of a Protest), refers, except when the **protest committee** decides either:

(a) rule 68.3 applies; or

(b) it was impossible for the yacht to have displayed a protest flag, because she was, for example, dismasted, capsized or sunk.

1.4 Unless the **protest** already provides the information;

Inquire whether the protestor tried to inform the protested yacht(s) (the protestee(s)) that a **protest** would be lodged (rule 68.4) and note his answer on the protest. Rule 68.4 is mandatory with regard to the attempt to inform, but not with regard to its success.

See that the protest fee (if any) required by the sailing instructions is included and note its receipt on the **protest**.

1.5 When the **protest** conforms to the requirements of rule 68, arrange to hold a hearing as soon as possible. Notify the representative of each yacht involved of the time and place of the hearing (rule 72.3 (Notification of Parties)).

1.6 The **protest** and any written statement regarding the incident (preferably photocopies) shall be available to all **parties to the protest** and to the **protest committee** for study before the taking of evidence. A reasonable time shall be allowed for the preparation of defence.

2 **The Hearing**

2.1 The **protest committee** shall ensure that:

(a) A quorum is present as required by the organising authority. The quorum is not affected when it is considered desirable that some members of the **protest committee** leave the hearing during the discussion and decision.

(b) No **interested party** is a member of the **protest committee** or takes part in the discussion or decision. Ask the **parties to the protest** whether they object to any member on the grounds of 'interest'. Such an objection shall be made before the **protest** is heard.

(c) When any member of the **protest committee** saw the incident, he shall only give his evidence as a witness in the presence of the **parties to the protest** and may be questioned.

(d) When a hearing concerns a request for redress under rule 69, (Requests for Redress), or rule 70.3, (Yacht Materially Prejudiced), involving a member of the race committee, it is desirable that he is not a member of the **protest committee** and would therefore appear only as a witness.

2.2 The **parties to the protest** or a representative of each (with a language interpreter, when needed) shall have the right to be present throughout the hearing. Each witness, unless he is a member of the **protest committee**, shall be excluded, except when giving his evidence. Others may be admitted as observers at the discretion of the **protest committee**.

2.3 Invite first the protestor and then the protestee(s) to give their accounts of the incident. Each may question the other(s). Questions by the **protest committee**, except for clarifying details, are preferably deferred until all accounts have been presented. Models are useful. Positions before and after the incident itself are often helpful.

2.4 Invite the protestor and then the protestee to call witnesses. They may be questioned by the protestor and protestee as well as by the **protest committee**. The **protest committee** may also call witnesses. It may be appropriate and prudent to ask a witness to disclose any business or other relationship through which he might have an interest in or might stand to benefit from the outcome of the **protest**.

2.5 Invite first the protestor and then the protestee to make a final statement of his case, including any application or interpretation of the rules to the incident as he sees it.

2.6 The **protest committee** may adjourn a hearing in order to obtain additional evidence.

3   Decision

3.1 The **protest committee**, after dismissing those involved in the incident, shall decide what the relevant facts are.

3.2 The **protest committee** shall then apply the rules and reach a decision as to who, if anyone, infringed a rule and what rule was infringed (rule 74, (Decisions and Penalties)).

3.3 Having reached a decision in writing, recall the protestor and protestee and read to them the facts found, the decision and the grounds for it (rule 74.7).

3.4 Any **party to the protest** is entitled to a copy of the decision (rule 74.7), signed by the chairman of the **protest committee**. A copy should also be filed with the committee records.

APPENDIX 7—Protest Form

To the Race Committee of .... Club

Race No. .... Class ....

Protest lodged by .... Sail No. ....

Against .... Sail No. ....

(whose helmsman I have/have not informed)

Date of incident .... Time of incident ....

Whereabouts of incident ....

Rule or rules considered infringed ....

Wind direction .... Force ....

Set of tidal stream or current .... Rate ....

Depth of water (if relevant) ....

Time at which protest flag was displayed ....

Time, if any, at which the protestor tried to inform the protestee that a

protest would be lodged ....

Signed .... Helmsman of ....

Member of .... Club

Address ....

    Tel. No: ....

Address during regatta ....

.... Tel. No: ....

Enclosed   : Protest fee

Witnesses

P.T.O.

Diagram submitted by ....
Show:—
(i)   The course to the next mark, or if close by, the mark itself, with the
          required side;
(ii)   The direction and force of the wind;
(iii)   The set and rate of the tidal stream or current, if any;
(iv)   The depth of water, if relevant; and
(v)   The positions and tracks of all yachts involved, prior to and at the
          time of the incident.
(vi)   Where possible yachts should be shown sailing from the bottom of
          the diagram towards the top.

Description of the incident.

....

....

Protest flag seen by .... (Race officer)

at ....

Protest committee .... (Chairman)

....

....

....

Facts found

....

....

Rule or rules judged applicable ....

Yacht holding right of way ....

Decision and grounds for decision

....

....

Signed ....

(Chairman)

Date ....

APPENDIX 8—Terms of Reference of an International Jury and Conditions for its Decisions to be Final

1. Constitution

An international jury shall consist of:

a chairman,
a vice-chairman,
a total membership, including the above, of not less than five nor more than sixteen, and in addition may include a secretary without a vote.

2 Membership

2.1 The membership shall be chosen and the officers appointed by the organising authority, subject to the approval of the national authority when it so requires, from amongst yachtsmen who have an intimate knowledge and experience of the racing rules.

2.2* A majority shall be international judges certified by the I.Y.R.U.

2.3 The international jury shall be separate from and independent of the race committee and shall not include any member of the race committee.

2.4 Not more than two (three when the event is held in Group L—SW Pacific) shall be from the same country.

2.5 When the numbers are reduced by illness or emergency and no qualified replacement is available, the jury shall remain properly constituted, provided that it consists of not less than three members, all from different countries (in Group L—SW Pacific, two may be from one country).

3 Functions

3.1 To make decisions on all matters relating to entries and to the measurement of yachts.

3.2 To direct the race committee to the extent provided by the organising authority in accordance with rule 1.5(d), (Authority for Organising, Conducting and Judging Races).

3.3 Either to amend or to authorise changes in or additions to the sailing instructions or other special notices issued to competitors.

3.4 To authorise the substitution of crews and yachts.

3.5 To hear and decide protests, as soon as practicable, in accordance with the principles of Appendix 6, (Protest Committee Procedure).

3.6 To take action, when deemed advisable, under rule 70.2, (Action by Race or Protest Committee).

3.7 To decide the extent to which the use of interpreters may be allowed.

3.8 To co-operate with the organising authority and the race committee, particularly on such matters as may directly affect the fairness of the competition.

4 Procedure

4.1 Decisions of the jury shall be taken by simple majority. Each member shall have one vote. When there is an equality of votes cast, the chairman of the meeting shall have a second or casting vote.

4.2* The jury may be divided into panels of not less than five members each, of which a majority shall be international judges. When a panel fails to agree on a decision, it may adjourn and refer the case to a meeting of the full jury.

5 Decisions

5.1 When the jury is properly constituted, there shall be no appeals from its decisions. The jury shall comply with rule 74.7, (The Decision). The jury remains properly constituted when it is considered desirable that some of its members leave the hearing during the discussion and the decision, provided that at least three members remain.

5.2 When the jury acts while not properly constituted, its decisions shall be subject to appeal to the national authority.

5.3 When approval of the jury is required by a national authority, its written consent for decisions to be final shall either be printed in the notice of race or regatta or in the sailing instructions or be posted on the official regatta notice board.

*During the inception of the international judges' programme, this requirement may be relaxed by the Permanent Committee each year and will be published in the Year Book. In 1985, the minimum requirement is two international judges certified by the I.Y.R.U. per panel, except in Group L where it is one judge.

APPENDIX 9—Excerpts from the International Regulations for Preventing Collisions at Sea, 1972.

At 1200 Zone time, July 15, 1977 the International Regulations for Preventing Collisions at Sea, 1972 came into effect in most waters of the world. Excerpts from these which might affect right of way between yachts *racing* when in effect in accordance with rule 3.2(b)(xxviii), (Race Continues after Sunset), are as follows:

Part A—General

Rule 3

General Definitions

(a) The word "vessel" includes every description of water craft, including nondisplacement craft and seaplanes, used or capable of being used as a means of transportation on water.

(b) The term "sailing vessel" means any vessel under sail provided that propelling machinery, if fitted, is not being used.

Part B—Steering and Sailing Rules

SECTION I—CONDUCT OF VESSELS IN ANY CONDITION OF VISIBILITY

Rule 4

Application

Rules in this Section apply in any condition of visibility.

Rule 5

Look-out

Every vessel shall at all times maintain a proper look-out by sight and hearing as well as by all available means appropriate in the prevailing circumstances and conditions so as to make a full appraisal of the situation and of the risk of collision.

Rule 6

Safe Speed

Every vessel shall at all times proceed at a safe speed so that she can take proper and effective action to avoid collision and be stopped within a distance appropriate to the prevailing circumstances and conditions.

Rule 7

Risk of Collision

(a) Every vessel shall use all available means appropriate to the prevailing circumstances and conditions to determine if risk of collision exists. If there is any doubt such risk shall be deemed to exist.

Rule 8

Action to avoid Collision

(a) Any action taken to avoid collision shall, if the circumstances of the case admit, be positive, made in ample time and with due regard to the observance of good seamanship.

SECTION II—CONDUCT OF VESSELS IN SIGHT OF ONE ANOTHER

Rule 11

Application

Rules in this Section apply to vessels in sight of one another.

Rule 12

Sailing Vessels

(a) When two sailing vessels are approaching one another, so as to involve risk of collision, one of them shall keep out of the way of the other as follows:

  (i)   when each has the wind on a different side, the vessel which has the wind on the port side shall keep out of the way of the other;

  (ii) when both have the wind on the same side, the vessel which is to windward shall keep out of the way of the vessel which is to leeward;

  (iii) if a vessel with the wind on the port side sees a vessel to windward and cannot determine with certainty whether the other vessel has the wind on the port or on the starboard side, she shall keep out of the way of the other.

(b) For the purposes of this Rule the windward side shall be deemed to be the side opposite to that on which the mainsail is carried or, in the case of a square-rigged vessel, the side opposite to that on which the largest fore-and-aft sail is carried.

Rule 13

Overtaking

(a) Notwithstanding anything contained in the Rules of this Section any vessel overtaking any other shall keep out of the way of the vessel being overtaken.

(b) A vessel shall be deemed to be overtaking when coming up with another vessel from a direction more than 22.5 degrees abaft her beam, that is, in such a position with reference to the vessel she is overtaking, that at night she would be able to see only the sternlight of that vessel but neither of her sidelights.

(c) When a vessel is in any doubt as to whether she is overtaking another, she shall assume that this is the case and act accordingly.

(d) Any subsequent alteration of the bearing between the two vessels shall not make the overtaking vessel a crossing vessel within the meaning of these Rules or relieve her of the duty of keeping clear of the overtaken vessel until she is finally past and clear.

Rule 16

Action by Give-way Vessel

Every vessel which is directed to keep out of the way of another vessel, shall, so far as possible, take early and substantial action to keep well clear.

Rule 17

Action by Stand-on Vessel

(a)   (i)   Where one of two vessels is to keep out of the way the other shall keep her course and speed.

     (ii)   The latter vessel may however take action to avoid collision by her manoeuvre alone, as soon as it becomes apparent to her that the vessel required to keep out of the way is not taking appropriate action in compliance with these Rules.

(b) When, from any cause, the vessel required to keep her course and speed finds herself so close that collision cannot be avoided by the action of the give-way vessel alone, she shall take such action as will best aid to avoid collision.

(c) This Rule does not relieve the give-way vessel of her obligation to keep out of the way.

Rule 18

Responsibilities between Vessels

Except where Rule 13 otherwise requires:

(b) A sailing vessel underway shall keep out of the way of:

     (i)   a vessel restricted in her ability to manoeuvre.

SECTION III—CONDUCT OF VESSELS IN RESTRICTED VISIBILITY

Rule 19

Conduct of Vessels in Restricted Visibility

(a) This Rule applies to vessels not in sight of one another when navigating in or near an area of restricted visibility.

(b) Every vessel shall proceed at a safe speed adapted to the prevailing circumstances and conditions of restricted visibility. A power-driven vessel shall have her engines ready for immediate manoeuvre.

(c) Every vessel shall have due regard to the prevailing circumstances and conditions of restricted visibility when complying with the Rules of Section I of this Part.

(d) Except where it has been determined that a risk of collision does not exist, every vessel which hears apparently forward of her beam the fog signal of another vessel, or which cannot avoid a close-quarters situation with another vessel forward of her beam, shall reduce her speed to the minimum at which she can be kept on her course. She shall if necessary take all her way off and in any event navigate with extreme caution until danger of collision is over.

Note—

These excerpts are not intended to be complete, but are intended to bring to notice the differences between these rules and those of Part IV of the Yacht Racing Rules. Please note that rules affecting sailing vessels are contained in the rules governing Lights and Shapes, and Sound and Light Signals.

APPENDIX 10—Weighing of Wet Clothing (Racing Rule 61)

Recommended Method

To test the weight of clothing and equipment worn by a competitor all items to be weighed shall be taken off and thoroughly soaked in water. Note: Equipment includes items such as trapeze harness, life jacket and heavy jacket.

The manner in which the clothing and equipment is arranged on the rack has a considerable effect on the weight recorded and it is important that free draining is achieved without the formation of pools of water in the clothing. It is recommended that a rack comprising "clothes hanger" type bars be used and that provision is made for suspending boots or shoes in an inverted position.

Pockets in clothing that are designed to be self-draining—i.e. those that have drain holes and no provision for closing them—shall be empty during the weighing; however, pockets or equipment designed to hold water as ballast shall be full when weighing takes place. Boots and shoes shall be empty when weighed.

Ordinary clothing becomes saturated within a few seconds but "heavy jackets" of the water absorbent type require longer and should be immersed for not less than two minutes.

On removal from the water the items shall be allowed to drain freely for one minute, at the end of which period the weight shall be recorded.

When the weight recorded exceeds the amount permitted, the measurer is recommended to allow the competitor to rearrange the clothing and equipment on the rack and then to repeat the test by re-soaking and re-weighing. When a lesser weight results, that weight shall be taken as the actual weight of clothing and equipment.

APPENDIX 11—Photographic Evidence

Photographs and video recordings may be accepted as evidence at a hearing and can sometimes be useful. However, there are some limitations and problems and these should be appreciated by the protest committee.

The following points may be of assistance to protest committees when video evidence is used, but many of them apply also to still photographs.

1   When a video recording is to be replayed to the protest committee by a party to the protest, he should arrange that the necessary machinery be set up in the hearing room and an operator (preferably the person who made the recording) be available to operate it.

2   The party bringing the video evidence should have seen it before the hearing and have reasons why he believes it will assist the committee.

3   It is usually preferable to view the video after the parties have presented their cases.

4   Allow the recording to be viewed first without comment, then with the comments of the party bringing the evidence, then with those of the other party. Questions may be asked in the normal way by the parties and the committee members.

5   The depth perception of any single-lens camera is very poor; with a telephoto lens, it is non-existent. When, for example, the camera's view is at right angles to the courses of two overlapped yachts, it is impossible to assess the distance between them. Conversely, when the camera is directly ahead or astern, it is impossible to see when an overlap begins or even if one exists, unless it is substantial. Keep these limitations firmly in mind.

6   Use the first viewing of the tape to become oriented to the scene. Where was the camera in relation to the yachts? What was the angle between them? Was the camera's platform moving? If so, in what direction and how fast? Is the angle changing as the yachts approach the critical point? (Beware of a radical change caused by fast panning of the camera.) Did the camera have an unrestricted view throughout? If not, how much does that diminish the value of the evidence? Full orientation may require several viewings; take the time necessary.

7   Since it takes only about 30 seconds to run and re-wind a typical incident, view it as many times as needed to extract all the information it can give. Also, be sure that the other party has an equal opportunity to point out what he believes it shows and does not show.

8   Hold the equipment in place until the end of the hearing. It is often desirable, during deliberation, to be able to review the tape to settle questions as to just what fact or facts it establishes. Also, one of the members may have noticed something that the others did not.

9   Do not expect too much from the videotape. Only occasionally, from a fortuitous camera angle, will it establish clearly the central fact of an incident. Yet, if it does no more than settle one disputed point, that will help in reaching a correct decision.

EXPLANATORY SECTION *(Red marginal marks)*

A third Fundamental Rule has been added. Rule 58 has been reclassified and now is Fundamental Rule A.

FUNDAMENTAL RULES

A. **Rendering assistance.** By bringing this rule into its new position more emphasis is given to the importance placed on racing yachts giving assistance to those in peril. Do not think that somebody else will look after the distressed vessel—you must attend the incident unless you are sure that your presence is no longer required. See IYRU Case 38. **122** **122**

B. **Responsibility of a Yacht.** The onus on whether or not a yacht *starts* must rest finally with the yacht and her crew.

C. **Fair Sailing.** For an example of this rule applying when *not* racing; a crew might deliberately damage a boat when racing. Because you can be disqualified between races it also means you could be disqualified for a whole series. Except for team racing a yacht is not allowed to receive outside help. There was a case where it was suspected that a crew was using a walkie talkie radio with another on shore. If it had been proved, then the yachts would have been disqualified. See also IYRU Case 107.

PART I—DEFINITIONS

Racing. The rules are in force from the preparatory signal (5-minute gun) until the boat has cleared the finishing line.

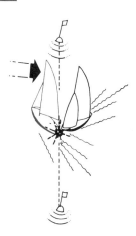

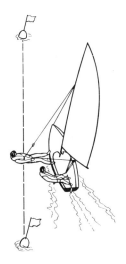

Even though the red boat has received her winning gun, she would be disqualified by black because she has not cleared the finishing line.

Definitions—Starting and Finishing

This boat has crossed the line to start. See also IYRU Case 34.

122

Definitions—Finishing

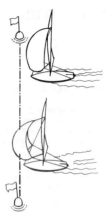

The rules say that the boat's crew has to be in his normal position. The red boat has not yet finished.

Red's spinnaker is not in its normal position and so she has not yet finished. See also page 119 for what happens when a boat touches a finishing mark. A further point to mention is that a race committee is not allowed to override the definition of finishing. See IYRU Case 102.

Definitions—Luffing and Tacking

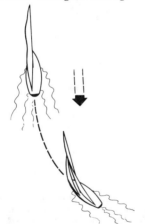

This yacht is luffing until she is head to wind. If she continues to turn she is tacking. See IYRU Case 77.

Note that the word 'luff' can also refer to a definite attempt to attack another boat by luffing. See Rules 38 and 40.

This boat finishes tacking when she reaches a close-hauled course on the new tack, even if the sail is not full because the main-sheet is too loose. Whether the boat has movement through the water or not is irrelevant. See IYRU Case 32.

Definitions—Tacking and Gybing

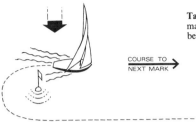

COURSE TO
NEXT MARK →

Tacking. This boat finishes tacking when her mainsail fills, which might be on any course between close-hauled and a broad reach.

This boat is gybing from the moment when her boom crosses the centreline until the time that the sail is full on the new gybe.

GYBING

Definitions—Clear Astern, Clear Ahead, Overlap

136

Watch out because a foresail, a spinnaker or a boomed-out jib could establish an overlap. The so-called 'transom line' is the critical overlap limit, but remember that it passes through the aftermost point of everything.

The Pink yacht is 'intervening' for the

purpose of Rule 38.6 (luffing two or more yachts), see page 90 and IYRU Case 59.

If Pink had been overlapping Red and Grey but on the far side of Grey, she would not have been an 'intervening' yacht under this definition.

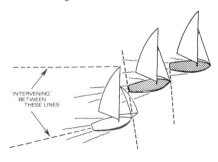

"INTERVENING"
BETWEEN
THESE LINES

Definitions—Clear Astern, Clear Ahead, Overlap

135

Overlap. Grey overlaps Red. There is no limit to the angle between the courses of Grey and Red, nor their distance apart, for an overlap to be valid, provided that the definition is satisfied. See IYRU Case 21.

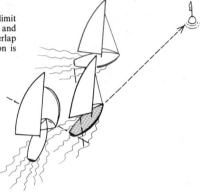

Clear Astern, Clear Ahead, Overlap. Red has not established an overlap because her spinnaker is not in the normal position.

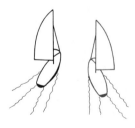

On the left, the definition says the boats are not overlapped. Rule 36 applies.

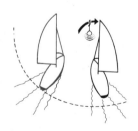

On the right, the boats are overlapped because Rule 42 applies.

Definitions—Windward Yacht, Leeward Yacht

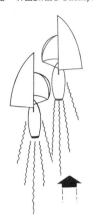

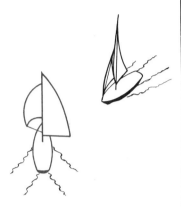

Because these yachts are not on the same tack, neither complies with the definition of windward yacht or leeward yacht.

Here, the definition is not strictly satisfied, but the boat nearer to the wind is the 'windward yacht'.

Definitions—Proper Course

122

The proper course is not necessarily the shortest course. There can be more than one 'proper course'. The criteria for a proper course is that the yacht should have a valid reason for steering that course and applies it with some consistency (IYRU Case 25). The end result has nothing to do with it.

Here, Grey can bear away to sail the curved course. See also Rules 38 and 39 and IYRU Cases 25, 62, 97 and 106.

122
136

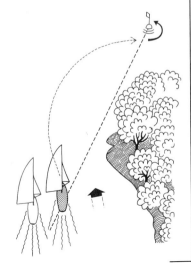

Definitions—Obstruction

123

A change of course is only substantial when a boat would lose a substantial amount of ground by altering course. A small fishing buoy, for example, would not cause any obstruction because it would just slide along the side of the boat without stopping it. Of course, even a small object such as a post or a buoy and objects such as weed, floating plastic or timber can still be an obstruction for the purpose of Rule 38.5 (Curtailing a luff). A racing boat is also an obstruction. See IYRU Cases 91 and 94.

PART II—MANAGEMENT OF RACES

122
123
139

3—The Sailing Instructions

Many clubs do not take enough trouble over Notices of Race and Sailing Instructions. This often results in confusion, disappointment and bad feeling. It is really very simple for clubs to go through Rules 2 and 3 and make out standard forms which can cover all races. Rule 3 says that the Sailing Instructions shall not alter Rules of Part I and IV and a few other Rules. However, anything else can be changed by them. Committees should be careful not to say too much. See also IYRU Cases 74, 75, 102.

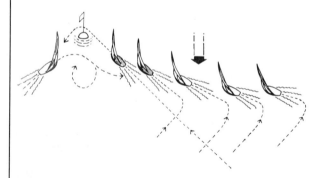

3.2 Contents of the Sailing Instructions. This drawing illustrates some of the problems for race committees and shows the likely situation when the weather mark is rounded to port.

The disadvantage of port rounding is that a boat approaching on port tack, even though she may be really leading as Red is here, may not be able to round the mark and can drop many places. Also, the tendency is to use only the starboard side of the course.

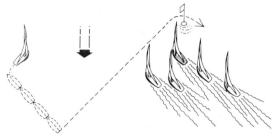

3.2 Contents of the Sailing Instructions.
With starboard rounding, a boat can always get round the mark by standing on a few lengths, but there are many more protest situations.

4—Signals

4.2, 4.3 and **5.1.** Always be prepared so that you can recognise signals in case the committee stops the race at one of the marks, shortens the course in a special way, or moves the windward mark as provided for in the programme. See the back cover of this book for quick reference.

4.2(a) SYSTEM 2. The White or Yellow, Blue and Red system of starting races, much used in American, is really very simple. It also gives boats one minute extra warning of the start since each shape is lowered one minute before the next is hoisted.

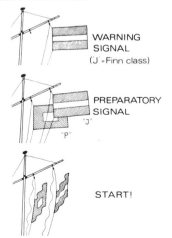

WARNING SIGNAL
(J'=Finn class)

PREPARATORY SIGNAL
"J"
"P"

START!

3.5 Oral instruction. Unless there is a special procedure laid down in the Sailing Instructions, the Sailing Instructions cannot be varied unless by written amendment. Oral instructions can easily be wrongly interpreted or even forgotten. See IYRU Case 125.

123

4.2(d) Signals for Starting a Race. If the race committee realises they have made the preparatory signal either too late or too early by mistake, they can do one of two things. They can either signal a 'General Recall' and start again, or they can continue with the start.

If they do the latter they must make sure that there is exactly the right time interval between the preparatory signal and the start signal, even if the preparatory was made late or early with reference to the warning signal (ten-minute gun).

4.5 Visual Signals to Govern. The timing is made from the flag and not from the gun, bell, whistle or hooter. See the drawing on the left and IYRU Case 70.

124

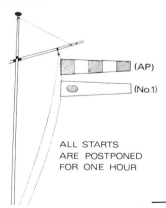

(AP)
(No.1)

ALL STARTS ARE POSTPONED FOR ONE HOUR

8—Recalls

The method of recall to be used must be made clear in the sailing instructions. The onus is on the yacht to see that it not only starts correctly (see also Rule 51.5) but also returns correctly if it is over the line at the starting signal. Unless it prescribes otherwise in the sailing instructions the race committee must make a sound signal for a recall (see IYRU Case 70), and support it with a visual signal or a hail.

13—Award of Prizes

You will often find that you will have to sign a declaration that all the rules have been observed correctly. If you forget to sign you will be disqualified. I would like to ask race committees not to ask for a declaration to be signed because, forgetting to sign has nothing to do with the result of the race, and a boat should not be disqualified for that. See also IYRU Cases 18 and 88.

PART III—GENERAL REQUIREMENTS

19—Measurement or Rating Certificates

With increasing regularity there are protests concerning these certificates. Owners must satisfy 19.2 in making sure that their yachts comply with the measurement certificates issued to them. Provided this is satisfied then they cannot be retrospectively invalidated after a race or series is completed. See IYRU Case 123.

21—Member on Board

When capsizing near the finishing line, a boat may finish with crew members in the water provided they remain with the boat. See IYRU Cases 1 and 90.

22—Shifting Ballast

Items of the boat's gear shall not be moved about to ballast the boat. Unless in use, gear must remain in its designated place.

Clothing and Equipment is Rule 61 on page 39.

PART IV—RIGHT-OF-WAY RULES

SECTION A—Obligations and Penalties

This is the most tricky part of the racing rules and so we will spend some time in examining cases in detail.

Remember that if you are racing and meet another yacht racing, these racing rules apply. It does not matter if the boats are in different races. If you are not sure that the other yacht is racing then the International Regulations for Preventing Collisions at Sea apply (otherwise known as 'Rule of the road at sea'), which all normal shipping has to recognise. These regulations always take precedence if there is doubt.

Take note that the IRPCS should always be enforced in a race between sunset and sunrise.

In order to settle any damage claims the result of a yacht racing protest is normally binding on two yachts racing. If one or both boats are not racing then liability depends on the 'Rule of the road at sea'.

Appendix 9 summarises the important and salient points of the IRPCS to assist competitors with this knowledge of the regulations.

31—Disqualification

Before you go afloat you should study the sailing instructions very carefully (see Rule 3) because you can be disqualified if you fail to keep any of the special rules for this particular race. For example, you may be required to carry some special flag in your rigging, or you may be required to wear life-jackets, or there may be some special starting instructions such as the one-minute rule, or you may have to carry extra buoyancy.

32—Avoiding Collisions

If the right-of-way yacht tries to avoid a collision and fails, and this collision results in 'serious damage', then she is in the clear.

But the problem is to decide what is 'serious damage'. There is not much that cannot be patched up quickly on a dinghy and it is the duty of the boat in the wrong to make amends as soon as possible.

Keelboats can do more damage to each other

but, on international race courses, the result of the race is much more important than the equipment. The collision only gives a more accurate indication of a protest situation.

IYRU Case 36 gives as a criteria for 'serious damage', whether the speed of the damaged yacht was markedly affected and her finishing position materially prejudiced. See also IYRU Cases 51 and 53.

124
125

33—Rule Infringement

If you are absolutely sure that you have broken a racing rule then you should either retire immediately or act under the alternative penalty arrangements if they are in force, but the racing rules have no way of stopping a man who has broken the rules from continuing. In such a case in points racing, you should not interfere with another competitor and force him to get a bad placing when your

own placing does not matter.

If you really have doubts as to who was right then you should put up your protest flag. If there was a collision, one or both yachts might have been wrong and it is best to find out that so you will know next time. See also IYRU Cases 2 and 13.

125

33.1 Accepting a Penalty. A yacht that acknowledges a rule infringement but does not

retire within a reasonable time shall be penalised. See IYRU Case 13.

125

122

33.2 Contact between yachts racing. If the contact is minor and unavoidable no action by either yacht is necessary, but beware – there are several interpretations of 'minor and unavoidable'. Should a third yacht make a protest under Rule 33.2 about the incident then it will be the job of the Protest Committee to decide. Further to this, a yacht which wishes to protect herself may make a protest under 33.2. If the Protest Committee decide at the hearing that contact was indeed minor and unavoidable then the protest may be withdrawn under Rule 68.9.

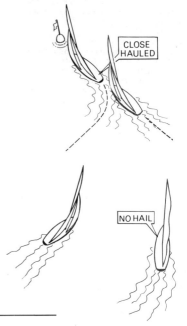

CLOSE HAULED

NO HAIL

34—Hailing

Examples of situations where hailing is required—
(1) Luffing a boat to windward of a mark.
(2) Right of way boat making unforseen course change likely to result in collision and serious damage.
(3) Tacking for room at obstruction.

137
125
134

34.2. This type of situation is covered by Rule 34. A hail from Black when she has completed her tack will clarify the moment when she gains the right to force Red to start avoiding a collision. See also IYRU Cases 55, 60 and 91 under Rule 42.3(c) and 112 under Rule 42.1(a)

No hail from Red tacking on to starboard may cause her to be disqualified for an unforseen alteration of course under Rule 34.1.

SECTION B—Principal Right of Way Rules and their Limitations

124
126
127

35—Limitations on Altering Course

Apart from the references mentioned below, IYRU Cases 36, 51, 86 and 115 are relevant.

35 and **41.**
Red has borne away to pass under Black's stern and Black decides to tack to cover. In order to avoid infringing Rules 35 or 41, Black must not tack until she is past the Red boat's course. There may be some doubt as to the actual direction of the course, and in this case the onus will be on Black to show that Red did not have to alter course further because of Black while Black's tack was in progress.

125
126

See also IYRU Cases 23 and 52.

CLOSE-HAULED COURSE

page

35 and **41.** Here Black bore away to pass under Red's stern. When Red saw this she tacked. There was a collision and Red was wrong under Rule 41 (Tacking boat keeps clear).

Rule 35 ceased to apply when Red passed head to wind and thus stopped being the right-of-way boat.

Red became right-of-way boat again when she completed her tack, but in such a case Black would not have to **begin** to take avoiding action until Red's tack was completed. See also IYRU Cases 10 and 23.

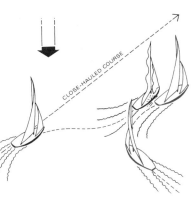

125

35 and **41.** If the Red boat luffs head to wind she can be disqualified under Rule 35 because Black had already altered course to avoid Red.

If she goes further and tacks, she can be disqualified under both Rules 35 and 41, depending on where the incident actually occurred. See also IYRU Cases 10, 23 and 53.

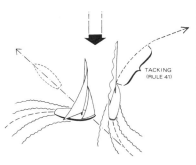

125
133

35. The Red boat, on port tack, has to remember that starboard tack boats like Black have the right to luff on to a proper course to start after the starting gun. Note that there is no proper course before the starting signal.

The timing of the signal and the boat's start can be quite far apart. Before the start, luffs (under Rule 40) have to be slow. But Black's luff here can be fast because the boats are on opposite tacks.

If this situation had occurred after Black had started it would be the same as if the marks were not there. Black could not luff to prevent Red keeping clear.

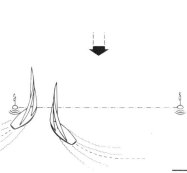

35. Red takes the mark rather wide and tacks. Black rounds tighter and can touch Red. Red is wrong under Rule 36 (Port and Starboard rule).

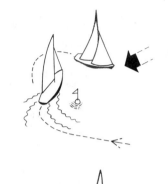

If the buoy has not been there, Black would be wrong under Rule 35 for obstructing Red who would otherwise have been able to keep clear. However, the final clause to Rule 35 (when rounding a mark) makes an exception in this case.

127

35—Limitation on Altering Course. If a right of way yacht alters course in such a way that the disadvantaged yacht in spite of prompt avoiding action still cannot keep clear by her own efforts then the right of way yacht infringes Rule 35. See IYRU Case 129.

124
125
126
127
128
131
133
134
136
137
138

36—Opposite Tacks—Basic Rule—Port and Starboard

Port and Starboard incidents without contact are very common. There is no requirement in the rules for the onus to be on the port tack yacht to prove he was clear of the starboard tack yacht, but conversely there is nothing in the rules to suggest that the starboard tack yacht should hit the port tack yacht. See IYRU Case 113.

IYRU Cases 6, 35, 36, 37, 45, 51, 52, 68, 71, 93, 112, and 113 contain further information on this rule.

36. Black has the wind coming from the starboard side and Red the wind from the port side. Thus Red should give way to Black.

125
126

36 and **35.** Red must not luff to try to hit Black, who would otherwise have been able to keep clear. This case comes under Rule 35. See also IYRU Cases 36 and 52.

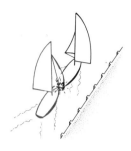

36. Even though Black is overtaking Red, the definition of 'clear astern' is not valid because they are on opposite tacks and so Rule 36 applies. Red must give way because Black is sailing on starboard tack.

36 and **42.2.** Here they are subject to Rule 42 and Red must keep clear even if Black gybes. See also Rule 37.2 and IYRU Cases 5 and 68.

133
131
136

37—Same Tack—Basic Rule

Some special cases are covered in IYRU Cases 3, 25, 45, 48, 50, 54 and 68.

122
128
129
130
131
132
135
136
137
138
143

37.1 When Overlapped. Red is windward boat and therefore has to keep clear of Black.

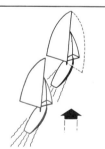

37.2 When not Overlapped. Red must keep clear and must not sail into Black's stern if they are on the same tack. See also IYRU Case 86.

127

37.3 Transitional. Before the start the Red boat comes from astern with better speed. Red obtained the overlap too close to Black, who was not given enough room by Red to luff clear. Black is right according to Rule 37.3. See also IYRU Cases 114 and 116.

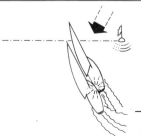

130
131

129   **37.3 Transitional.** In this special case Red has overtaken Black but has given too little room for Black to be able to luff and keep clear, because Black's stern will swing to port as she luffs. See also IYRU Cases 11 and 46.

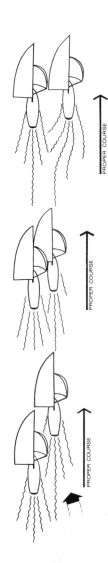

37.1 and **37.3 When Overlapped and Transitional.** The Black yacht is overtaking. From the moment that Black gains an overlap the Red boat becomes the 'windward yacht'. She must then start to luff far enough so that Black does not touch her boom, but she need not luff any further because Black must not luff above her proper course. See IYRU Cases numbers 11, 27, 46 and 106.

122
129
137

38—Same Tack—Luffing and Sailing above a Proper Course After Starting

IYRU Cases 3, 4, 48, 58, 60, and 62 are relevant.

38.1 Luffing rights. Red is overtaking. Black has the right to luff because she was ahead and is now to leeward, and is still ahead of Red's 'mast abeam' position.

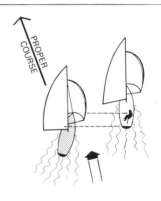

38.1 Luffing rights. Pink is overtaking Black but on a course which is slightly higher than the proper course. We cannot talk about luffing here, but nevertheless Black's helmsman should call 'Mast abeam!', and thus Pink is obliged to turn back on to the proper course and may not luff again as long as this overlap exists. See also IYRU Case 24 and and Rule 40 for this situation before starting.

132

38.2 Proper Course Limitations. Red establishes her overlap by diving through the Pink yacht's lee but must not luff above her proper course whilst the overlap lasts. If there is a dispute about what is the proper course then the Pink yacht must keep clear. See also IYRU Cases 25 and 106, and also our interpretation of Proper Course.

122

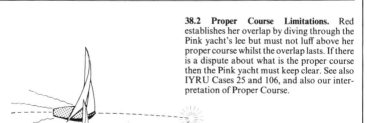

PROPER COURSE

38.3 Overlap Limitations. The measurement of the two boats' length distance is taken from hull to hull as shown, but this maximum limit only applies to Rule 38 (Luffing).

Rule 39 (Bearing away) has a three length limit.

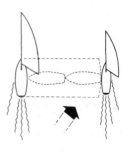

38.3 Overlap Limitations. At the start the overlap begins at the time when the leading boat actually crosses the starting line.

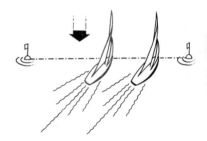

38.3 Overlap Limitations. Black's overlap starts from the moment when she completes her tack. Here the Black yacht overlaps the Red.

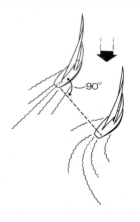

38.3 Overlap Limitations. Black is overtaking Pink and as soon as her mast goes forward of Pink's helmsman, she may gybe and then gains luffing rights. If Black was overtaking on the same gybe as Pink, then she could gain her luffing rights by doing two quick gybes. But see IYRU Case 35.

38.3 Overlap Limitations. The overlap starts from the moment the boats have completed their gybes and therefore there can be no question of luffing rights until this moment. See IYRU Case 62.

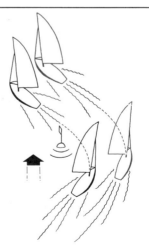

38.4 Hailing to stop or prevent a Luff.
Remember to call 'Mast abeam!' or something similar, because this is the only way you
can take away the luffing rights of the leeward
boat. After this the leeward boat must bear
away on to her proper course. She can only
regain luffing rights if she breaks the overlap
by drawing clear ahead or more than two
lengths abeam, and then re-establishes it
again with her mast forward of the windward
boat's helmsman. See also Rule 40 and
IYRU Cases 3, 4 and 101.

129
131
132

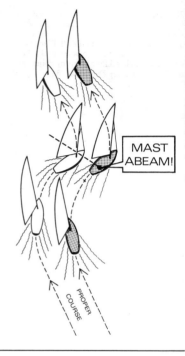

MAST
ABEAM!

PROPER
COURSE

38.4 Hailing to stop or prevent a Luff.   Red
starts to luff correctly but hits Black when she
is obviously behind the mast abeam position.
Red is wrong. There is no doubt because the
position of the collision proves it.

However, Black did not hail 'Mast abeam!'
and should have kept clear under Rule 37.1
and so she is also wrong in this case.

The only way to stop Red luffing is to hail
'Mast abeam!'. If there is doubt it is Red's
risk to continue. There is a big difference between continuing luffing and and actual contact. See also IYRU Cases 48 and 99.

130
131
132
143

page

38.5 Curtailing a Luff. Pink is entitled to luff and does so in this case. Red can now stop the luff by calling 'Water'. Pink does not have to return to her proper course but need only just give enough room, because Red has not reached 'Mast abeam!' position. See IYRU Case 106.

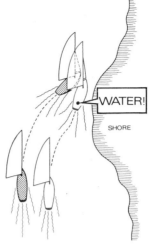

122

38.6 Luffing two or more yachts. In this instance, Red has luffed the others, but because of her turn, loses luffing rights over Pink. Pink can call 'Mast abeam!' and force Red to go back on to her proper course. See also IYRU Case 4.

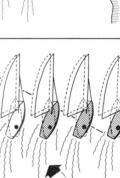

132

38.6 Luffing two or more yachts. The Pink yacht is 'intervening'. Red must respond to a luff from Black, who has rights over Pink and Red. Red must also allow room for Pink even though Pink may have no luffing rights of her own over Red.

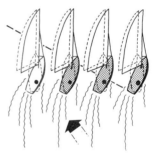

39—Same Tack—Sailing Below a Proper Course After Starting

39. Black is inside a distance of three boats' lengths from Red. Red must not bear away from her proper course to interfere with Black if it is a free leg of the course.

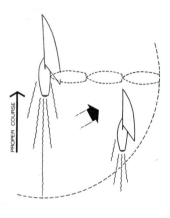

PROPER COURSE

39 and **37.1.** If the leg is to windward, Pink may bear away towards Black's course, but if she touches she will be disqualified under Rule 37.1. If a tack will have to be made to reach the next mark this is evidence that the leg is to 'windward'. See IYRU Case 106.

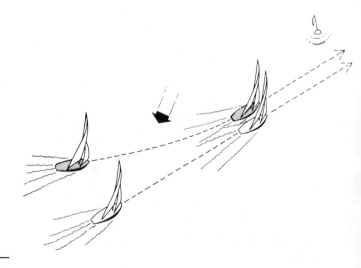

40—Same Tack—Luffing Before Starting

40. Provided Black is ahead of 'Mast abeam!' position she can luff slowly head to wind. She cannot be forced to bear away at any time before or after the starting signal. See also page 83 lower drawing. IYRU Case 115 is relevant in a match racing situation.

126

40. As long as Black is not ahead of the mast abeam position he may only luff slowly to a close hauled course. She must give Red enough time and room to keep clear. See IYRU Case 24.

132

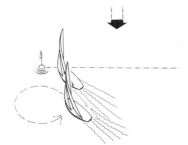

40. Red must not luff above close-hauled to squeeze round the mark, when she is aft of 'Mast abeam!'. See also Rule 43.3.

41—Changing Tack—Tacking and Gybing

41.1, 2 and **3 Basic Rule, Transitional and Onus.** Red tacks on to starboard and must have completed her tack before she can claim right-of-way over Black. Black does not have to begin to give way until Red's tack is complete. See also the example on page 102 (top) and IYRU Cases 32, 53 and 58.

122
125
131
132
133

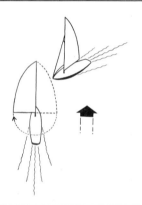

41.1, 2 and **3 Basic Rule, Transitional and Onus.** Red must complete her gybe before she can force Black to alter course. Here Red has gybed too late to gain right-of-way over Black, because Black has no possibility of being able to keep clear. In case of doubt the onus of proof is on Red. In practice this means that Red must have a witness from a third boat.

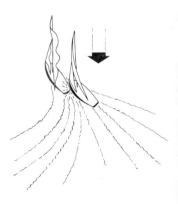

41.2 Transitional. Red is coming on port tack and is tacking on to starboard tack. Red has only just completed her tack. Black does not have to start to luff until after this moment and is therefore right. See definition and IYRU Case 32.

122
132

Note: 41.3. Onus. It is clearly stated in this rule, and applies also to other rules, that you have to 'satisfy the race committee' that your manoeuvre was correct. Unless you can succeed in this your whole case will fail.

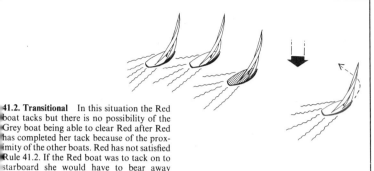

41.2. Transitional In this situation the Red boat tacks but there is no possibility of the Grey boat being able to clear Red after Red has completed her tack because of the proximity of the other boats. Red has not satisfied Rule 41.2. If the Red boat was to tack on to starboard she would have to bear away astern of the Grey boat.

41.2, Transitional and **42.** In this situation if the Black yacht (on the right) tacks, the Red boat can only bear away (and give room to Pink and Grey under Rule 42 if they have an overlap). This is because there is no time for the Red boat to hail Pink and Grey for room to tack themselves before a collision would occur with Black.

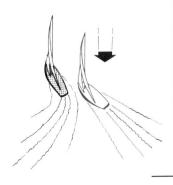

41.3. Onus Red protests. It will be easy for Pink to satisfy the committee because there was no collision. Red must remember that she must touch Pink in order to have a good chance of winning the protest. This is a sensible interpretation because it is too easy for Red to put in a protest in cases like this. If Red can touch Pink without bearing away he ought to win the protest. Red does not have to being to luff clear until Pink's tact complete.

41.4 When Simultaneous. In each case the Red yacht, which is on Black's port side, must give way. Remember it like this 'If you are on the right—you are right!'.

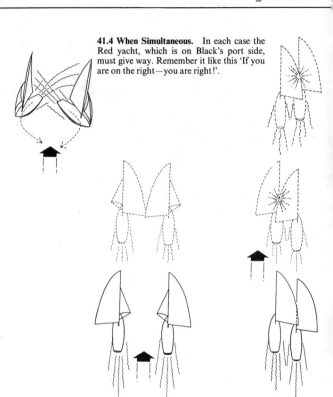

SECTION C—Marks and Obstructions and Exceptions to Section B

All Rules in this section cover special cases. When these cases apply they override all the basic rules which precede them in Section B of Part IV, with the exception of Rule 35 which has its own limitations.

Section A (31–34) rules always apply and do not describe the sort of boat-to-boat situations covered in Section B (35–41) and Section C (42–46).

42—Rounding or Passing Marks and Obstructions

This is one of the most important rules as it is the one that is involved most frequently.

42.1. Instructions for rounding and passing marks and obstructions when *overlapped* either as an inside or an outside yacht.

42.2. Instructions for rounding and passing marks and obstruction when yachts are *not*

overlapped either when clear ahead or clear astern.

42.3. Exceptions and Limitations.

42.4. The special case of room at a starting mark.

42(a). This clause says that Rule 42.1(a) does not apply in this situation because the two boats are sailing to windward on opposite tacks. Rule 36 applies, and so Black does not have to give room to Red to round a mark inside her.

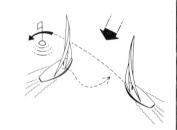

42(a). Red cannot claim room during her tacking manoeuvre though she may have rights both before and after it.

It is exactly the same as if they were on the open sea with no mark anywhere near. Rule 41 would apply in such a case.

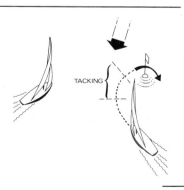

TACKING

page

42—Rounding or Passing Marks and Obstructions

42.1—When overlapped

42.1(a). An Outside Yacht. Red shall give room to Black, assuming Black made her overlap in time. See also Rule 42.3 for the limits to claiming overlaps, and IYRU Case 50.

130
135

42.1(a) An Outside Yacht. Black must have enough room to be able to gybe without being obstructed by Red. Red must still keep clear even if Black's gybe breaks the overlap. See also IYRU Case 5.

133

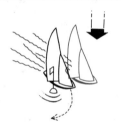

42.1(a) An Outside Yacht. Black, the inside overlapping yacht, must have room to be able to tack. If Black's genoa touched Red when it was freed off for the tacking, for example, Red would not have given enough room. See also IYRU Case 40 for an interpretation of the word 'room'.

135

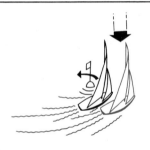

42.1(a) An Outside Yacht, and **43.** The starboard tack boat is an obstruction. Red can elect to tack or to bear away. If the latter, she has to give room to Pink who is overlapping 'inside'. IYRU Cases 6 and 20.

134
138

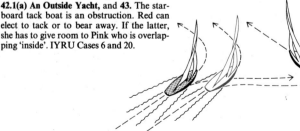

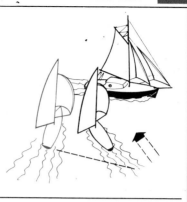

42.1(a) An Outside Yacht. The boat not racing is crossing the course and Red must give Black room to pass on the same side as herself.

Also when approaching a mark Red must give Black room even though both yachts are on widely differing courses. See also IYRU Case 21.

135

42.1(e) An Inside Yacht. Red, unless she has luffing rights, must gybe on to her proper course. Black can choose what she does. This rule overrides Rule 37. See also IYRU Case 62.

136

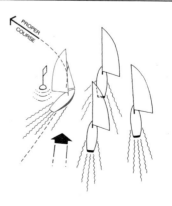

42.1(e) An Inside Yacht. Red must gybe on to the new proper course at the earliest opportunity. She is not allowed to continue and force the others to keep clear. This Rule overrides Rule 36.

42.1(a) An Outside Yacht. When a yacht comes abreast of a mark but is more than two lengths from it, and when her alteration of course towards the mark results in a yacht previously clear astern becoming overlapped inside her, Rule 42.1(a) requires her to give room to that yacht. See IYRU Cases 5 and 127.

133
134

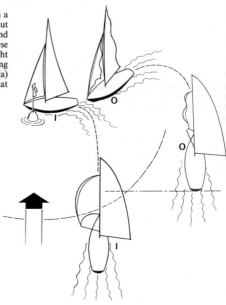

42.1(b) An Outside Yacht. It may sometimes happen that, when sailing in strong currents, one or both boats may drift outside the two-length zone before rounding. If only the inside boat drifts outside the circle then the overlap still technically exists. If the outside boat drifts outside then the overlap has to be re-established. See IYRU Case 71.

128
136

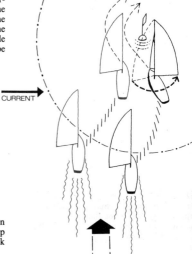

CURRENT

42.1(b) An Outside Yacht. Black has an overlap in time. The gybe breaks the overlap but this rule says that in this situation Black can still claim room to round inside.

42.2—Rounding—When not Overlapped

42.2(a) A Yacht Clear Astern. Black, who is clear ahead, has the right to gybe. This is part of the rounding manoeuvre and so Red must stay clear until Black has gybed and cleared the mark.

See also the top, right drawing page 85 and IYRU Case 68.

131
136

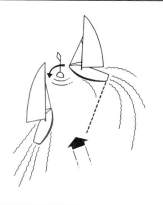

42.2(a) A Yacht Clear Astern. Red must keep clear even though she now has an overlap because this was not made in time (see Rule 42.3(a)). Neither can Red claim her starboard tack rights.

This clause covers the case of a gybe. A tack is covered in paragraph (c).

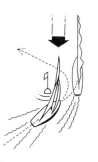

42.2(c) A Yacht Clear Ahead, and **41.** Red is clear ahead but cannot claim room to tack because 42.2(c) says that in this case Rule 41 is the correct rule. See IYRU Cases 17 and 26.

123
136

42.2(b) and (c) A Yacht Clear Astern. If Black thinks she is far enough ahead to be able to tack and clear Red without causing her to alter course, she can do so. Red must not then luff above a close-hauled course to prevent Black from clearing her.

This is really a small extension of Rule 35. It means that the mark should be ignored.

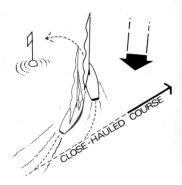

42.2(c) A Yacht Clear Astern. The course is from a reach to a reach. Grey luffs nearly head to wind. White cannot get between Grey and the mark because of Rule 42.2(a). After White has steered to pass under Grey's stern then Grey can tack and continue.

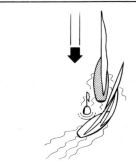

42.3—Exceptions and Limitations

42.3(a). We all know how boats surge back and forth relative to each other on waves. This can be quite dangerous when claiming room at a mark and so you have to claim your overlap before the leading boat is within two lengths of the mark. This gives her a fair chance of giving room.

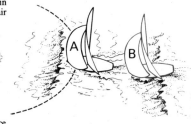

B is too late. She is surfing on a wave at twice the speed of A who has no chance of giving room.

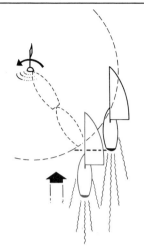

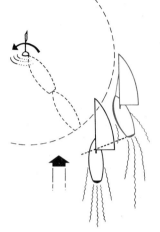

42.2(a). Black is allowed to make a normal smooth rounding. She is within a radius of two boat lengths of the mark and is also clear ahead of Red, and so she does not have to give room when she is altering course to round the mark.

42.3(a). Red is not within the limit distance of two boat lengths of the mark when she alters course, so she cannot refuse to give Black room.

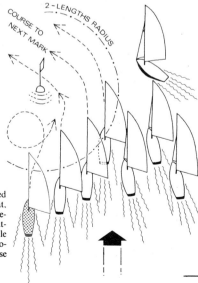

42.3(a)(i). Even though Pink has established an overlap in proper time on the next boat, the latter may not be able to give room because of the delay in response from the outside boats. If she has been given too little room, Pink ought not to risk making a protest under Rule 42.2(a). See also IYRU Case 27.

103

42.3(a)(ii) Limitation on Establishing an Overlap. In this case 42.1(a) applies since there is no question of obtaining an overlap from **clear astern**. Black's tack has been completed within the circle. The circle can therefore be forgotten and Black can try to obtain room under 42.1(a) or 37.1.

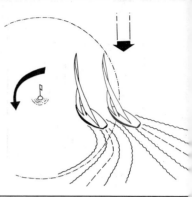

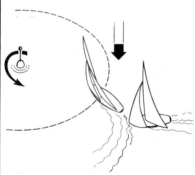

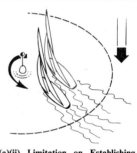

42.3(a)(ii) Limitation on Establishing an Overlap. Red had completed her tack within the circle. Black would have right-of-way before the tack (36), during the tack (41) and after the tack (37.1) but had to respect 37.3. The two-length limit does not apply and Black can try to get room with a late overlap.

135
136

42.3(a)(ii) Limitation on Establishing an Overlap. Red completes her tack within two lengths of the mark. Therefore Black can ask for room between Red and the mark. See IYRU Case 59.

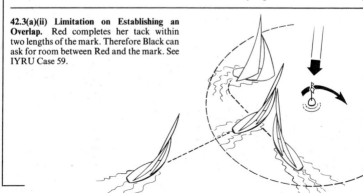

42.3(b) Limitation when a Obstruction is a Continuing One. This is an awkward Rule to interpret. Presumably the leading boat is already as close to the obstruction as she thinks she can go with safety. Therefore it is difficult for the overtaking boat to show that she can go safely closer. See IYRU Case 69.

The two-lengths limit does not apply so it is dangerous to try for an overlap under this rule. If an overlap is established correctly, Pink cannot luff Red ashore.

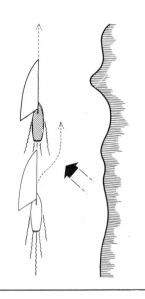

137

42.3(c) Taking an Inside Yacht the Wrong Side of a Mark. Black wants to take Red to windward of the mark. She must hail 'Luffing to windward of the mark!' and also start to luff outside the two-lengths circle.

Black cannot then go back and must also pass a line through the mark perpendicular to the last course, A (IYRU Case 55). However, if Red tacks away first, B, Black does not have to go to this line. See IYRU Case 61.

137
138

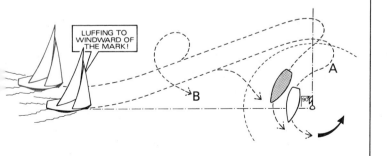

LUFFING TO
WINDWARD OF
THE MARK!

A

B

90°

42.3(b) Limitation when an Obstruction is a Continuing One. Black must be careful when arriving at a break in the obstruction. This is Red's chance to establish an overlap.

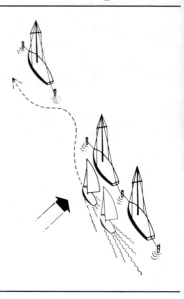

128 **NOT 42.3(a) Limitation on Establishing an Overlap.** This case was the subject of IYRU Case 45. Black, on starboard tack, has right-of-way over the other two. The windward port tack boat is not a 'continuing obstruction' with respect to the others.

137
127 See also IYRU Case 67 for another situation where 42.3(b) does apply, and also IYRU Case 35.

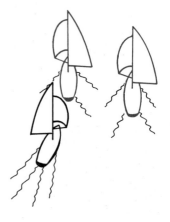

42.4—At a Starting Mark Surrounded by Navigable Water

42.4. The Red boat can neither claim room between White and the mark before the starting gun not afterwards. Rule 37.1 also applies.

The Grey boat, which is ahead of 'Mast abeam', is head to wind and has the right to do this also after the starting gun has fired because Pink has plenty of room between her and the mark. See IYRU Case 54.

This rule is often called and 'anti-barging rule'.

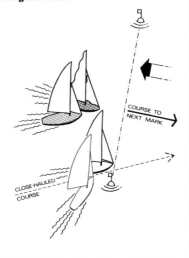

129
138

42.4. As soon as the starting gun has fired, Grey must bear away onto the course for the first mark and must not squeeze White out by sailing higher than this.

If there is still not enough room for the White yacht then Grey is not obliged to sail lower than the course to the first mark. 42.1 does not apply but 37.1 does. See IYRU Case 54.

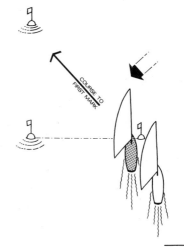

129
138

43—Close-hauled, Hailing for Room to Tack at Obstructions

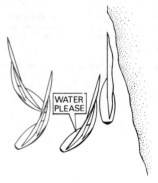

43.1 and .2. Hailing and Responding. Black can no longer continue in safety. Red must start to tack immediately she hears Black's hail. Black must start to tack before Red has completed her tack.

43.1 and .2(b). Hailing and Responding. Black was the right to call for water, but Red can reply 'You tack!', and then she is obliged to keep clear of Black. Black must start to tack immediately after Red's reply hail.

Red must remember that in the case of a protest she will have to prove that she has kept clear of Black during this manoeuvre.

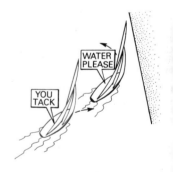

138

43.1 Hailing. In this case Red is easily able to tack and keep clear of Black. She has no right to call for water. She only has the right to call for water when she is certain that she cannot clear Black either by passing ahead, or by bearing away under her stern. See IYRU Cases 80 and 117.

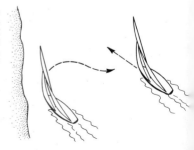

43.1 Hailing.   Grey shall hail for room to tack and Red must keep clear.

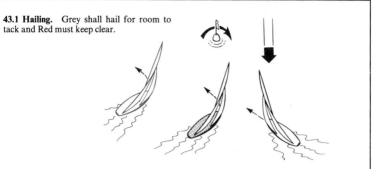

43.1 Hailing.   Here Black shall hail and Red must tack, not because she cannot lay the mark (43.3), but because Grey is coming in on starboard tack.

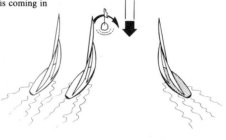

43.1 Hailing.   Grey shall hail Red for room to tack.

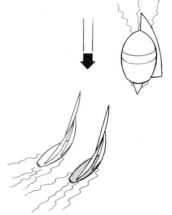

43.3—Limitation on Right to Room to Tack when the Obstruction is also a Mark

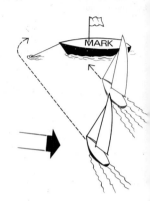

43.3(a). If Black can fetch the mark she need not give Red room to tack unless Red cannot avoid a collision either with the mark or with Black. Then Red should hail a second time and immediately she is clear she must retire.

If Red had been slightly more to windward she would have been able to hail for water because of the mooring rope which is not part of the mark (see definitions).

43.3(b).
Case 1. The line is between two buoys. The starting boat is not a starting mark.

In this situation Black can hail Red for room to tack at any time. Red can only hail Grey for room to tack because of the starting boat and not to pass the right side of the starting mark. If Black were not there Red might have been forced to sail over the line between the mark and the starting boat before she could claim room.

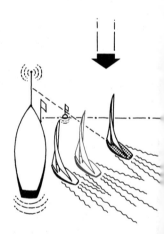

43.3(a)
Case 2. The starting boat is a starting mark, as is the inner limit mark, which has a 'required side' only after a yacht starts (i.e. first cuts the line after the gun).

Neither Black nor Red can claim room to tack from Grey when the obstruction is a starting mark.

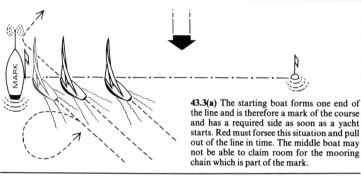

43.3(a) The starting boat forms one end of the line and is therefore a mark of the course and has a required side as soon as a yacht starts. Red must forsee this situation and pull out of the line in time. The middle boat may not be able to claim room for the mooring chain which is part of the mark.

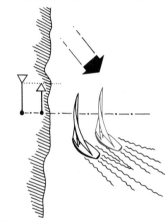

43.3(b). In the case of a starting line transit which is completely on the shore, both before and after the start Black can hail Red for water to tack because the shore is an obstruction.

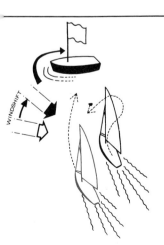

43.3(c). After Red has declined Black's call to tack, the latter bears away in order to tack and pass under Red's stern. Now the wind shifts and Red cannot any longer lay the mark. Because of her refusal Red must immediately retire.

44—Returning to Start

44.1. Even though a boat which has started too early is on starboard tack, she has to keep clear of all others—even port tack boats.

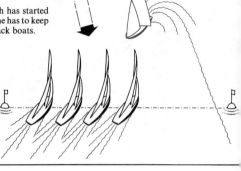

44.1. Red has started too early and luffs into the wind in order to slow down so that she can drop back and start again. But if she affects the Grey boat, then Grey will have to respond and Red will be disqualified.

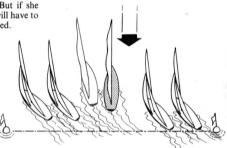

44.1. The Red boat has started too early but the only thing she can do is let go the jib and the mainsail. She can slow down by backing the sails if she can do it without affecting the other boats.

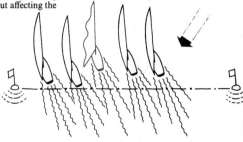

44.1. As soon as the starting signal is made, the Red boats, who are on the wrong side of the line, must keep clear. Before the starting signal has fired they have right-of-way because they are on starboard tack, but as they have to gybe or tack before they can start, and while making this manoeuvre keep clear, it can be dangerous to start in this way.

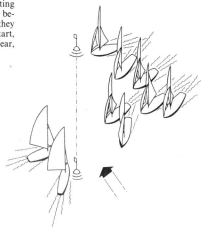

44.1(b). Even though she has regained her starboard tack rights, the Red yacht must tack or bear away because the rule says that she has to give the Grey boat, for example, ample room and opportunity to keep clear. It will be impossible for Grey to comply in this situation.

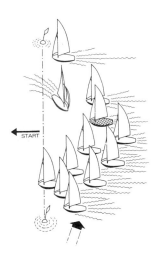

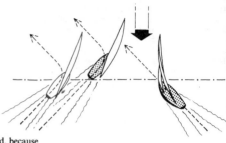

138

44.2. Pink has started too early and, because of the starboard tack boat, she has to call upon Red for room to tack. Pink has the right to do this because she is not yet returning to make her restart. After tacking she can then begin to slow down as long as this does not affect Black or Red. See IYRU Case 81.

139

45.1 Re-rounding after Touching a Mark. If you are re-rounding a mark to exonerate your touching it, you must give other yachts rounding the same mark, without penalty, room to do so. Rule 42.1(a) is not applied. But yachts making a normal rounding may not take advantage of the offending yachts; they must round in the normal way and assume their proper course. Rule 35 applies. See IYRU Case 126.

46—Person Overboard; Yacht Anchored, Aground or Capsized

46.1. You have to keep clear of a capsized dinghy. Under the rules it is the same as if it was an obstruction.

46. Pink, on starboard, was hit by Red, on port, and knocked on to the other tack. Pink is now nearly stopped on port tack and is hit by Black who is on starboard.

Boats 'out of control' are not covered by this rule. Pink is not wrong and should protest against Red.

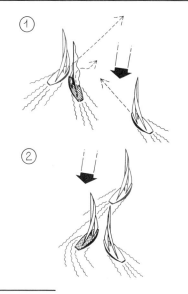

PART V—OTHER SAILING RULES

51—Sailing the Course

During a normal start a yacht which is over the line early can restart like the white yacht. However, if the 'round-the-ends' Rule 51.1(c) is involved and Code flag 'I' is flown, as frequently happens after a general recall, then a yacht which is over the line will have to return like the Grey yacht.

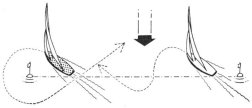

51.1(a) Sailing the Course. Inner and Outer limit marks described in the Sailing Instructions as being part of the Finishing line must be either on the line or on the course side of the line. If a limit mark is laid or drifts to the post-course side of the Finishing line, it should be disregarded. See IYRU Case 124.

139

51.1(a). If the sailing instructions say that you should finish by leaving the committee boat to port and, for example, if they put the committee boat on the wrong side of the mark, you should follow the finishing definition exactly. See IYRU Case 102.

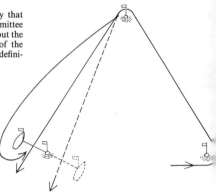

51.3. Both marks 1 and 2 are marks of the course for boat A.

B has just rounded mark 2 and therefore mark 1 is no longer considered as a mark for her.

C has not yet rounded mark 1 and therefore she can please herself which side of mark 2 she goes. She can touch it without infringing these rules (see Rule 52).

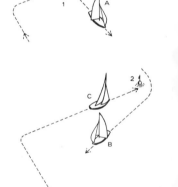

51.2 and .4. Red has rounded incorrectly. Black is right. You have to unwind yourself before rounding properly.

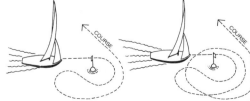

51.3. A starting mark first has a 'required side' when a boat starts (i.e. first cuts the line), but it must not be touched even before the start.

A starting limit mark first has a 'required side' when a boat is approaching the line to start.

This definition is not clear unless it means 'after the starting signal' because a boat does not 'approach the line to start' until then.

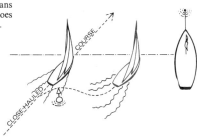

51.3. Black must be correct because she has passed the limit mark on the required side when approaching the line to start.

Red is wrong because the mark had already been passed before her 'approach to the line to start'.

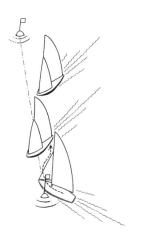

51.5. Red, who has crossed the finishing line, still has to keep clear of the starboard tack boats. She can go under their sterns and still maintains her finishing position because she has already finished. She may clear the line in any direction.

52—Touching a Mark

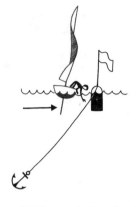

52 and **definition—mark.** You can touch the buoy rope with the keel without infringing Rule 52 unless it is a Starting Mark. See Rule 43.3(a) when the ground tackle *is* part of the mark. If you foul the rope and it is caught round the keel or rudder you can use your own gear to clear it. See also Rule 55.

52 and **definition—mark.** Even though the mooring rope is not considered part of the mark unless it is a Starting Mark it is still forbidden, under Rule 55, to use the anchor line as a means of avoiding touching the mark.

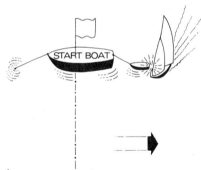

52 and **definition—mark.** You can touch the dinghy tied up at the stern without fear of penalty.

141

52.1 Touching a Mark. Once you have hit the mark you must do one of three things. Either exonerate yourself under 52.2 Re-rounding the mark, Protest under Rule 68 or exonerate yourself by accepting an alternative penalty when laid down in the sailing instruction. See IYRU Case 120.

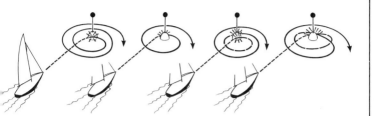

52.2. After touching the mark, all these tracks will correct the error according to this rule.

The key to what has to be done is:
1. The mark has to be rounded or passed according to the sailing instructions (forgetting about the touching) until the boat is on the new proper course.

2. The penalty rerounding runs from this point until the boat has passed through a further 360°. The manoeuvre ends when the boat is on its new proper course.

Rule 45 says that a rerounding boat has no rights of way until that moment. See also IYRU Cases 64 and 126.

139
141

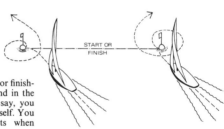

52.2(b) and **45.** If you hit a starting or finishing line mark you can only reround in the direction shown here. That is to say, you must start before exonerating yourself. You must keep clear of other boats when rerounding.

A boat rerounding a finishing mark does not finish until she cuts the line for a second time.

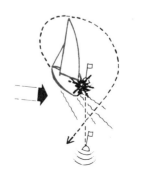

52.2. According to the definition—racing, and rule 51.1, if this boat touches the mark, even after she has crossed and cleared the finishing line, she has to reround and does not finish until she crosses the line a second time.

119

53—Casting Off, Anchoring, Making Fast and Hauling Out

All of the boat, including the anchor, must be behind the line when kedging before the start.

54—Means of Propulsion

54.1(b). The rule makes it abundantly clear that you may not gain speed by roll tacking. You must not exit from a tack faster than you went into it. That means that roll tacking in light winds is forbidden.

142

54.1(d). It is plain that in kedging or anchoring you must drop your anchor immediately by the yacht and not throw it forward. In recovery you cannot haul it up with such speed that the yacht gathers way sufficient to pass ahead of the spot at which you dropped your anchor. See IYRU Case 9.

54.2 and **54.3**. It is written quite clearly now that no continuous movements or actions are allowed except that you may pump three times only down the face of a wave and that you may ooch on the wave but that is all. Once you are off the wave there can be no more movement until you are on the next.

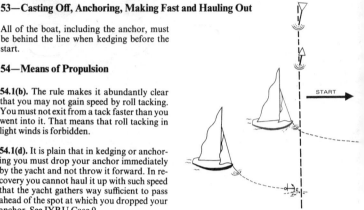

58—Boarding

124
142

If a boat loses a man overboard she may receive help or assistance from another competitor or spectator boat as long as no forward progress is made during the recovery operation. See IYRU Cases 1 and 66.

61—Clothing and Equipment

In the final paragraph of Appendix 10 a competitor whose weight of wet clothing and equipment exceeds the amount permitted may rearrange the clothing and equipment on the draining rack and repeat the test. This may be interpreted as reweighing the clothing and equipment piece by piece.

62—Increasing Stability

Crews racing in off-shore yachts equipped with upper and lower lifelines are permitted to have the upper part of their bodies outside the upper lifeline when sitting on the deck facing outboard.

64—Setting and Sheeting Sails

64.2. Be careful how you fix your jib fairleads so that they do not contravene this rule, but a hand holding out a sheet is not an outrigger. See IYRU Case 7.

68—Protests by Yachts

68.2 Protest flag. The flag must be flown as soon as it is practicable following an incident. A protest is not lodged until it is written on paper and handed to the race committee. Do not be afraid to fly the protest flag if you are in any doubt. You may find when you get ashore that it is not necessary to continue with the protest, in which case you do not have to lodge it. See IYRU Case 47.

68.4 Informing the Protested yacht. A protesting yacht must attempt to inform the protested yacht but it is not mandatory that she succeeds in the attempt. However, you must convince the Protest committee of your attempts. See IYRU Cases 92 and 104.

68.5 Protest to be in writing. A yacht that is involved in an infringement but which she believes is not her fault must nevertheless lodge a written protest herself. See IYRU Case 41 under Rule 52.1.

69—Requests for Redress

The Race Committee cannot be protested by a yacht. The yacht may seek redress only when she alleges that her finishing position has been materially prejudiced. Neither can the Race Committee be expected to know the class rules for each class that is racing. Think of the problems they would have in a multi-class regatta. See IYRU Cases 45, 88, 95 and 119.

70—Action by Race or Protest Committee

70.4 Measurer's Responsibility. The measurer referred to in this rule is the measurer appointed specifically for that race or series of races. He is not the measurer of the National authority or the Class measurer (unless of course he has been specially appointed for that race or series of races). See IYRU Case 123.

77—Appeals

77.1 Right of Appeal. A yacht may appeal only if she has been party to the Protest. If she was not party to the Protest, but affected by the decision and wishing to raise the matter she must seek redress under the terms of Rule 69. See IYRU Case 119.

IYRU Interpretations to the Racing Rules

FUNDAMENTAL RULES

73 | **A. Rendering Assistance**
IYRU Case 38. Rendering assistance. Rendering assistance to those in peril is compulsory to those in a position to do so. It does not matter that help may not have been asked for, nor that subsequently it may be shown not to have been needed.

73 | **C. Fair Sailing**
IYRU Case 23. The Fundamental Rule cannot be invoked unless no other rule applies. See also Case 53.

IYRU Case 107. A yacht that deliberately hails 'Starboard' when she is on port tack has not acted correctly and is liable to disqualification.

PART I—Definitions

73 | **Starting** | *IYRU Case 34.* To rank as a starter a boat must either start, or sail about
73 | | near the line between the preparatory and starting signals. Some scoring
74 | | systems may include additional boats not in the area at the time.

| **Finishing** | *IYRU Case 102.* The finishing definition cannot be over-ruled by a Sailing Instruction (Rule 3.1). There is no provision for allowing dispensation for other methods of finishing (Rule 5.1(a)). See also IYRU Case 1.

124 | **Tacking** | *IYRU Case 32* states that when beating, a yacht has completed her tack
74 | | when she is heading on a close hauled course, regardless of her movement
75 | | through the water, or the sheeting of her sails.

| | *IYRU Case 77.* In attempting to pass a mark by shooting head to wind, a yacht inadvertently passed beyond head to wind and then back again. She was, by definition, in the act of tacking and, having collided with another yacht while doing so, is disqualified under Rule 41.1.

77 | **Proper Course** | *IYRU Case 25.* An interpretation of 'proper course' is that there is a logical
122 | | reason for it and that a yacht sails it with some consistency. When, owing to a difference of opinion as to proper course, two yachts on the same tack converge, Rule 37.1 applies. See also Case 97 below.

| **Proper Course** | *IYRU Case 97.* A leeward yacht L had no luffing rights over W and based her alteration to a converging course on a temporary spinnaker problem which, she claimed, caused this higher, converging course to be a faster course to the next mark, and hence a 'proper course' for her.
It is correct that new conditions may cause a new proper course to be justifiable, but also that consistency is an essential part of a proper course which cannot be ordinarily or temporarily changed.
In particular a leeward yacht, without luffing rights, is not entitled to use a temporary problem of poor seamanship or sail handling to justify a luff. Since L was aft of 'Mast Abeam', Rule 38.2 applies. See also Case 25.

122 | **Proper Course** | *IYRU Case 106* refers to two yachts on converging courses approaching the finishing line. In the absence of W, L would have luffed to finish at right angles to the line, but W wished to sail dead downwind to finish at the starboard end of the finishing line. L did not have luffing rights

However Rule 37 says that when two yachts on the same tack are overlapped then the windward yacht shall keep clear, but that L is limited by Rules 37.3 and 38.2. From the evidence it seemed that L's proper course was correct, and provided that she fulfilled 37.3 and 38.2 she could reasonably assume her proper course, but not luff above it.

Proper Course
IYRU Case 17. Nowhere in the rules is a yacht required to sail a proper course. In tacking round a windward mark a yacht must comply with Rule 41 and thereafter with Rule 36.

77

Marks and Obstructions
IYRU Case 94. An island begins and ends at the water's edge. When used as a mark, the part below water does not count as a mark. A protruding jetty or rock would be part of the mark. A yacht going aground below the water's edge would not infringe Rule 52.1(a).

Obstruction
IYRU Case 91. W and L, who are overlapped, are overtaking A, all on the same tack. A ranks as an obstruction to W and L. When either comes within 2 lengths of A Rule 42 starts to apply. W or L can elect to pass their respective sides of A under 42.1(a) and must allow room to the other to do so as well. There is no obligation to hail, though it could be helpful to do so (Rule 34.2).

78

PART II—Management of Races

Rule 3.1
IYRU Case 74. Sailing Instructions changing the IYRU Rules. The course instructions of Rule 5 were varied without specific reference as required by Rule 3.1. This omission is incorrect and, in addition, in this case a yacht was materially prejudiced. A protest under Rule 69 correctly resulted in the race being abandoned and re-sailed. See also IYRU Case 102.

78
79

Rule 3.2(b)(xxviii)
IYRU Case 87. Racing after Sunset. Between sunset and sunrise the International Regulations for Prevention of Collisions at Sea (IRPCS) replace the IYRU Rules, Part IV. IYRU Definitions are also not applicable to the wordings of the IRPCS. IRPCS Rule 17(a)(i) effectively prevents the 'racing' manoeuvre known as 'luffing', for example. IRPCS phrases such as 'near proximity' have no precise meaning and should be understood in terms of what might, in the circumstances, be seamanlike behaviour. See IYRU Appendix 9—Excerpts from IRPCS.

122
139

Rule 3.5
IYRU Case 75. Sailing Instructions and oral briefing. The Sailing Instructions cannot require a competitor to attend an oral briefing. He is entitled to expect all necessary information to be contained in the Written Sailing Instructions, possibly with amendments made in accordance with Rules 3.4 or 3.5.
In this case a yacht was materially prejudiced and can take action under 69 (not 68.1 which can only be invoked between two yachts) and there is no requirement therefore to show a protest flag.

79

Rule 3.5
IYRU Case 125. Sailing Instructions and Oral briefing. Before the first race of a series several competitors forget to collect their 'tally boards' before going afloat. The Race Officer permitted this to be corrected by radio.
On the following day this facility was refused when the protesting yacht had sailed three quarters of the course. She was disqualified and appealed. The appeal was dismissed. The Sailing Instruction was mandatory; and

79

in going racing without a tally board, the competitor had contravened the Sailing Instructions.

79 | **Rule 4.5**

IYRU Case 70. Signals at the start. Under this rule the timing only of starting signals is governed by the visual signal. There must also be a sound signal but it need not be made at the same moment.

Rule 5.1(b)

IYRU Case 85. Cancelling—each race is separate. During the progress of a race the Race Committee may decide under Rule 5 to cancel one or more races in a regatta at its discretion. In this case the RC acted under provisions of 9.1(b) when a mark was missing but cancelled all the races. Subsequent protests to the Jury should only affect those races from whose Competitors protests had been received. Race Committee decisions on other races should stand.

Each race in a multiple regatta is a separate race and should be considered separately.

Rule 5.1(b)

IYRU Case 110. A Race Committee is not entitled to abandon a race on account of a windshift, unless so prescribed in the sailing instructions.

Rule 13

IYRU Case 18. Declarations or not, and Rule 13. Even though declarations may not be required the Race Committee should satisfy themselves that all the Rules, Sailing Instructions and Class Rules have been observed and take action under Rule 70 if necessary.

80 | **Rule 13**

IYRU Case 88. Declarations and Class Rules. Rule 13 can only be invoked by the Race Committee. It is normally unreasonable to expect a RC to be familiar with Class Rules and so competitors should protest directly if they have complaints under this heading. RC's discretion may not be questioned on appeal and it is not obliged to apply Rule 69 in such circumstances.

PART III—GENERAL REQUIREMENTS

80 | **Rules 18, 20, 21**

IYRU Case 90. Entries, ownerships, helmsman. Unless specifically stated in the notice of the race and for the Sailing Instructions the owner, or person in charge, is free to decide who steers a yacht in a race provided Rules 20 and 21 are complied with.

80 | **Rule 21**

IYRU Case 1. Member on board. Finishing a race while capsized and with one or more crew swimming alongside satisfies this rule, provided the whole crew remains with the boat.

PART IV—RIGHT OF WAY RULES

Section A—Obligations and Penalties

81 | **Rule 32**

IYRU Case 51. Avoiding collisions. Two boats in different races were rounding the same mark in opposite directions. Rule 36 applied. P was disqualified. S was also disqualified for failing to avoid a collision which resulted in serious damage.

Rule 32   *IYRU Case 36. Serious Damage.* In considering whether damage was serious thought should be given to the extent and cost of reinstatement relative to the size of the boat and whether it was feasible or prudent for her to continue racing; and if so, whether the damage markedly affected her speed and materially prejudiced her finishing position.

The wording of Rule 32 does not penalize a right of way yacht which touches another which should have kept clear.

81

Rule 32

IYRU Case 53. Avoiding Collision and disqualification. A leeward (L) yacht on port tack tacked without warning and W had no time or warning to avoid a collision and the Protest Committee found this as a fact. W cannot be held to be wrong in such a case. Note that disqualification under Rule 32 is not automatic.

81

Rule 33.1   *IYRU Case 2. Accepting penalty.* A yacht which is disqualified during a race, but continues, can subsequently protest over a later incident.

81

Rule 33.1   *IYRU Case 13. Retiring promptly.* Two yachts on port tack PW and PL were caught by a starboard tack boat, S, which had to duck their sterns to avoid a collision. PL had hailed PW to tack but had received no reply. She therefore protested PW under Rule 43.2(a). PW did not realise she was being protested until after the race, when she promptly retired. However, the protest committee heard the protest and disqualified PW under 43.2(a) and 33.1.

Rule 34   *IYRU Case 91. Hailing.* There is no obligation to hail for room at a mark or obstruction. A yacht need take no such action though a hail could be helpful in supporting a claim under Rule 42 if a protest followed.

82

Section B—Principal Right of Way Rules and their Limitations

Rule 35   *IYRU Case 10. Close-hauled tacking and keeping clear.* When sailing to windward P bore away to pass astern of S. S, however, tacked. P resumed her course after S had completed her tack. There was no collision. P's alteration in course does not of itself mean that S cannot also do so. In this case Rules 41 and 35 were complied with so no one was at fault.

82

Rule 35   *IYRU Case 23. Obstructing the right of way yacht.* P bore away to pass under the stern of close-hauled yacht, S. S immediately tacked and the swing of her stern caused P to have to bear away further, so infringing Rule 35 and also 41.1.

82

82
83

Rule 35

IYRU Case 52. Obstructing after benefiting from a wind-shift. A close-hauled starboard tack yacht luffed to take advantage of a wind shift. P would have been able to cross clear ahead of S before the shift. In this case S was still able to keep clear by bearing away so no rule was infringed. It was S's responsibility under Rule 35 not to prevent P from keeping clear.

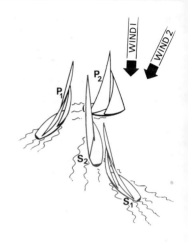

82
83
84

Rule 35

IYRU Case 36. Trying to hit an opposite tack yacht. Rule 35 always applies and over-rides Rule 36. A right of way starboard tack yacht may not try to hit a port tack yacht.

Rule 35

IYRU Case 115. In a typical match racing pre-start manoeuvre one yacht drives another yacht away from the starting line. Yachts A and B reached away from the starting line on port tack. A moving faster passed B and became clear ahead. As A luffed to tack so B luffed with her, preventing A from tacking. A then bore away to gybe but B bore away to leeward of her and prevented her from gybing. Rule 35 applies only to a right of way yacht which B was not, either in positions 3 or 4. In position 4 B as windward yacht had to keep clear under Rule 37.1 and as A could not tack without infringing 41.1. At position 5 B was leeward yacht and then held rights under Rules 37.1 and 40.

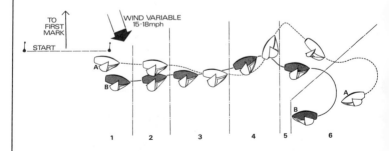

Rule 35
IYRU Case 129. Right of way yacht altering course. Port tack yacht A rounded the windward mark to starboard and immediately gybed onto starboard. Instead of running downwind to the next mark she decided for tactical reasons to reach away at right angles to the course. As she luffed to her new course she came bow to bow with yacht B on port tack still making for the mark. B bore away fast but it was not sufficient and A had to luff sharply as well to avoid the collision. There was no contact. A had no right to luff abruptly into the path of B for whatever reason; tactical desires do not relieve a yacht of her obligations under the Rules. A was disqualified for infringing Rules 35 and 41.2.

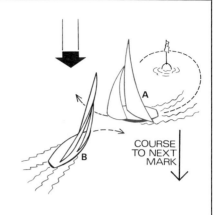

Rule 35(b)

IYRU Case 86. Limitations on altering course before the start. Rule 35 does not alter basic rights. Its purpose is to protect a yacht that has to give way from being obstructed in fulfilling this obligation.

In this case B (Behind) was following A (Ahead) during pre-start manoeuvring, including A bearing away and then luffing to assume her proper course to start. During the latter action B touched A's stern and protests under Rule 35. B should have anticipated A's action in luffing to assume proper course and is wrong under Rule 37.2. A did not mislead B.

Rule 36
IYRU Case 35. Basic Port/Starboard rule versus Rule 35 (limitations on altering course). W and L were running, overlapped, on port gybe for some time. W gybed onto starboard. She then hailed L and started to luff up slowly. The yachts touched. As a fact it was found that she did not, in this case, infringe Rule 35 and so Rule 36 applies.

Rule 36 also takes precedence, on opposite tacks. S overtakes P from astern. P must keep clear.

84
85

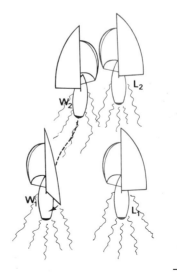

Rule 36   *IYRU Case 37. Rounding marks in opposite directions.* Whether by accident or design, in such cases Rule 36 applies. The yachts were not 'about to round the mark on the same side' and so Rule 42 does not apply. See also Case 51 below.

Rule 36   *IYRU Case 51. Rounding marks in opposite directions.* Rule 36 applies (see Case 37). The rules are primarily framed to avoid collisions. In this case P also failed to keep a good lookout and the resulting collision was serious (see Rule 32).

Rule 36   *IYRU Case 45. Three running yachts, one of them on Starboard tack.* S overtook two port tack yachts, which were less than two lengths apart, and intervened between them. Rule 36 applies. There is no question of the port tack yachts being 'obstructions' to S since Rule 42 does not apply. See also Case 45 under Rule 42.3(a).

Rule 36
IYRU Case 71. Tacking round a mark in a heavy wind. Rule 42.3(a) (and 42.2(a)) applies only to a yacht clear astern provided that the yacht clear ahead does not tack. A tacks and, provided she satisfies Rule 41, Rule 36 applies.

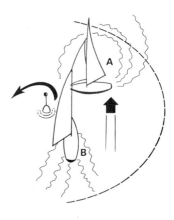

Rule 36
IYRU Case 113. In a straightfoward port and starboard case a protest committee must inquire carefully into whether the starboard tack yacht did actually bear away to avoid collision, or that there was genuine and reasonable apprehension of collision. If this was so, then the port tack yacht should be disqualified.

Rule 36
IYRU Case 93. Approaching a continuing obstruction on opposite tacks. P was sailing close-hauled close to, and parallel with, a continuing obstruction. S approached on a collision course. P should keep a good lookout and anticipate such an incident since Rule 36 applies to opposite tack yachts. P must keep clear.

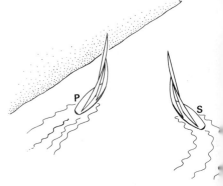

Rule 37.1
IYRU Case 3. A windward yacht shall keep clear of a leeward yacht. L luffs W correctly until W calls 'Mast Abeam'. Whereupon L bears away suddenly to her proper course. In doing so, her tiller extension touches W. W has failed to give L sufficient room and is disqualified.

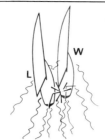

Rule 37.1

IYRU Case 54. Windward and Leeward yachts at a starting mark. The anti-barging Rule (42.4) and the windward/leeward Rule (37.1) can, and usually do, apply at the same time since they are complementary. Rule of exception only takes precedence when there is conflict.

Rule 37

IYRU Case 11. Overtaking to leeward. When running towards a mark, L steered a course to overtake W and pass to leeward. The moment L established an overlap, W became subject to 37.1. L at the same time became bound by 37.3 and had to allow W room and opportunity to keep clear.

L, now being behind Mast Abeam position was also subject to Rule 38.2 and could not sail above her proper course. In this case, when approaching the mark, L luffed slightly and touched W. It was established that the luff was justified as being an alteration to a new proper course and W was therefore wrong under 37.1.

Rule 37

IYRU Case 46. Overtaking to leeward. On establishing a leeward overlap Rule 37.2 ceases to apply. The windward yacht then becomes bound by 37.1; the leeward yacht by 37.3.

'Ample room and opportunity' to keep clear includes any action such as luffing head to wind if she pleases. If A touches B in so doing then B has not given enough room. B's obligation under 37.3 is not a continuing one, however.

Rule 37

IYRU Case 24. Converging courses before starting. A steady converging course, without luffing, does not infringe Rule 40. Rule 37.1 applies.

ule 37
'RU Case 27. Yachts overtaking
'erlapping yachts clear ahead and at-
mpting to intervene. If the yachts
ear ahead are close together Rule
·.3(b) may apply, in which case the
achts clear astern are prohibited
om making overlaps on them.

ssuming that there is room for a
·cht clear astern to pass between
vo yachts clear ahead in safety,
ule 37 applies.

·hen X establishes an overlap on A
·e is bound by 37.3; A by 37.1.
hen Y establishes an overlap on D
·e is bound by 37.1. Y has no right
· way between C and D.

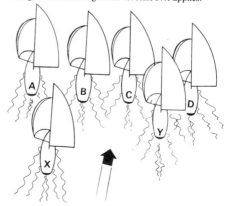

IYRU Interpretations

Cross-reference pages

page

85
86

Rule 37

IYRU Case 48. Luffing rights—three overlapping yachts. In this case the yachts were fairly level at one stage, M having luffing rights over W, and L having luffing rights over W and M. Later W drew ahead and bore away somewhat, to go for the mark, touching M, with her stern to M's bow.

It was obvious that M had lost her luffing rights over W at this stage but there was doubt whether L had still retained her luffing rights. W did not hail 'Mast Abeam'.

M was not entitled to luff W therefore L was entitled however to continue to sail above her proper course, since there was doubt about her right to luff W, and M had to respond, as intervening yacht, and to keep clear of L under 37.1.

91
132

W infringed 37.1 by failing to keep clear and was disqualified. See also Case 48 under Rule 38.6.

85
86

Rule 37

IYRU Case 50. When a mark has been 'passed'. W and L were passing a leeward mark. L gave W adequate room but W was slow in rounding the mark and sheeting in her boom. The Protest Committee found as a fact that W did not round the mark and come up to a proper course as soon as she could do so and there was contact.

It was clear that W and L had passed the mark and that there was no reason for W to sail below her proper course. Rule 42 had ceased to apply. Basic Rule 37.1 applied. W was disqualified.

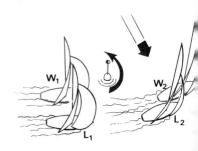

Rule 37.1

IYRU Case 116. Immediately before a start W was dead in the water with sails flapping. L approaching from leeward, established an overlap and hailed 'Leeward boat'. W took no evasive action until after L had borne away. No contact was made. W clear ahead need not anticipate her obligation to keep clear before being overlapped to leeward from clear astern. Neither yacht was penalised as no rule was infringed.

130

Rule 37.1 *IYRU Case 114.* In a situation where there are intervening windward yachts being prevented from luffing clear of a leeward yacht, the intervening yachts must do all they can to persuade the windward yacht to keep clear either by luffing or hailing or both.

Rule 37.2 *IYRU Case 68. Overtaking at a continuing obstruction.* A line of running starboard tack boats were sailing one behind the other close to, and parallel with, a continuing obstruction, the shore.

85
86

Boats clear astern are required, under Rule 37.2, to keep clear of boats clear ahead.

The leading boat now gybes on to port but Rule 36 is overridden because they are all subject to the rule of exception, 42, since they are passing an obstruction on the same side. The gybe therefore makes no difference to the terms 'clear ahead' and 'clear astern' which apply here to boats on opposite tacks. Rule 42.2(a) therefore applies and boats clear astern must still keep clear.

Rule 38 *IYRU Case 58. Luffing—limits and intentions.* Two boats are sailing close-hauled; L, to leeward and ahead cannot tack without infringing Rule 41 but, forgetting this she starts to do so. W hails and L returns to her close-hauled course fast. The boats touched however.

87
88
89
90
122
91

The Protest Committee found as a fact that at no time did L pass through head-to-wind. Therefore, in spite of her admitted original intention to tack, she correctly used her right to luff under Rule 38. W should have kept clear under Rule 37.1. See also IYRU Case 106 under Definition of Proper Course.

Rule 38 *IYRU Case 60. Luffing—hailing requirements.* A leeward yacht, with luffing rights, can luff as hard and as suddenly as she pleases without any warning or hail, provided she is on open water.

When 'about to round or pass a mark' Rule 42.3(c) applies and a hail is required together with the other requirements of this rule.

Rule 38.2 and 38.4 *IYRU Case 101. Hailing for 'Mast Abeam'. Cases of doubt. Normal station.* Decisions in this Appeal include: A hail which is not heard is inadequate and must be repeated. In a case of doubt that 'Mast Abeam' position had been reached, L has the right to luff as she pleases and Rule 37.1 applies. 'Normal station' can vary, even among yachts of the same class.

Rule 38.4
IYRU Case 99. 'Mast Abeam'—a case of doubt. W overtook L at nearly twice her speed. L luffed and W responded. At 'Mast Abeam' W stopped responding but L continued to luff and there was contact in such a position that it was obvious W was ahead of 'Mast Abeam'. Rule 38.2 therefore applies. Rule 38.4 only applies in cases of doubt.

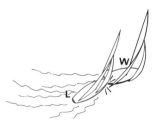

Rule 38

IYRU Case 4. Luffing rights with three yachts. L correctly luffs M and both yachts converge on W who was sailing faster and had reached 'Mast Abeam' by the time they were two lengths apart. There was no hail.

L now had no right to luff under Rule 38.2 and was required to turn back to her proper course. However, L continued to luff and M fouled W. W should have called for 'water' under Rule 42.1(a). W should have protested against L. See also Case 4 under Rule 42.1(a).

132

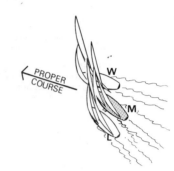

91   **Rule 38.6**

IYRU Case 48. Luffing rights—three yachts. Luffing rights include th right to sail above a proper course. When 'Mast Abeam' position reached, the leeward yachts must return to a proper course but, if ther is doubt W is not entitled to bear away. She is subject to Rule 37.1, an must also respond under Rule 38.6 to a luff from an intervening yach which has no luffing rights over her, but which is herself required unde Rule 37.1 to keep clear of a leeward yacht. See also Case 48 under Rul 37.

130

93   **Rule 40**

IYRU Case 24. Converging courses before the start. During pre-start manoeuvring L reached a position to leeward and astern of W but was sailing faster. L then sailed a steady converging course on W, gaining an overlap to leeward in the process. The Protest Committee found as a fact that W had ample room and opportunity to keep clear. L did not luff and so Rule 40 did not apply. There was contact and W was disqualified under Rule 37.1.

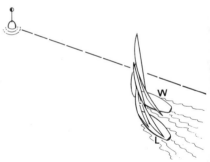

93   **Rule 40**

IYRU Case 98. Luffing before the start. Before the start W and L wer overlapped with W further ahead. L hailed and started to luff. W responded. L luffed more but W claimed she could not respond furthe without swinging her stern against the side of L. L therefore bore away. Neither yacht infringed any rule, W because she kept clear to windwar (Rule 37.1), and L because she bore away when it became obvious sh was not giving W enough room to keep clear of her luff (Rule 40). Se also IYRU Case 115 under Rule 35.

126
94
95

96   **Rule 41**

IYRU Case 32. Definition of 'Tacking'. A yacht completes her tack whe she reaches the new close-hauled course. Movement through the wate and sail sheeting are irrelevant.

Rule 41

IYRU Case 23. Tacking too close. P bore away to pass astern of S, b S immediately tacked and thereby caused P to alter course further to avo her. S infringed Rule 41.1 (and also Rule 35).

Rule 41   *IYRU Case 53. 'Anticipation' and 'Time to respond'.* L, on port tack, tacked without warning on to starboard and hit W immediately after her tack was completed. Even though, in the circumstances, W knew that L was about to tack for the mark, she did not have to anticipate that she would have to give way. She only had to start to take action when L's tack was complete. As with many other rules, time for response is allowed which starts only after the moment right-of-way is actually established.

Rule 41   *IYRU Case 93. Close handed on opposite tacks near an obstruction.* A port tack close-hauled yacht which is sailing close to leeward of an obstruction must be prepared to avoid a starboard tack yacht which has satisfied Rule 41 and is approaching on a collision course.

Rule 41   *IYRU Case 98. Gybing during pre-start manoeuvres.* Gybing close to windward of another yacht before the start does not infringe Rule 41 when the other yacht does not have to alter course.

Section C—Marks, obstructions and exceptions

Rule 42.1(a)   *IYRU Case 4. Luffing rights with three yachts.* L, who has luffing rights over M, luffs M until she collides with W. L and M have no luffing rights over W at this point who has drawn ahead of 'Mast Abeam', though no hail was given.

When a collision seemed imminent, M should have called for 'Water' on L under Rule 42.1(a).

Rule 42.1(a)

IYRU Case 5. Clear ahead and clear astern at mark. Outside yacht (O) gybed from port to starboard when level with a starboard hand mark but several lengths to the side of it. The inside yacht (I) was on port tack, but clear astern just before O's gybe, but was within two lengths of the mark. O must now keep clear of I, even when I gybed and became clear ahead of O during the rounding. 42.1(a) overrides 37.2.

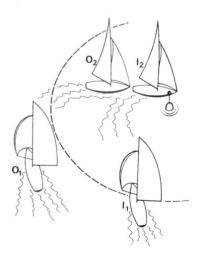

Rule 42.1(a)

IYRU Case 127. Four yachts in line abreast are running towards a mark on port. A fifth yacht B is just clear astern of the line of four. The two inside yachts A1 and A2 gybe on to starboard and round the mark to port satisfactorily. The outer two yachts A3 and A4 still lie outside the two length circle as they start their gybe, and B gybes inside them, now within the two length circle. By Rule 42.3(a)(ii) B is entitled to room around the mark under Rule 42.1(a).

97
98
99

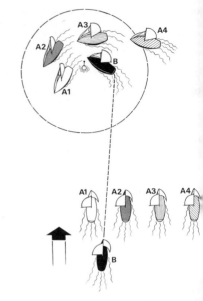

Rule 42.1(a)

IYRU Case 20. Another yacht racing is an obstruction. W and L, overlapping, close-hauled on port tack approach S, close-hauled on starboard tack. W can ask L for room to bear away to pass astern of S. She is not obliged to tack. IYRU Case 112 also refers.

97
98
99
134

Rule 42.1(a)

IYRU Case 112. Two yachts, PL and PW are broad reaching in a lot of wind on port tack. They are on a collision course with yacht S which is beating to windward on starboard tack. S is an obstruction to PW under 42.1(a) who required room from PL to avoid a collision. There was contact of rigging between S and PW. Rule 36 required the port tack yacht to keep clear but PW was unable to, because PL did not give sufficient room. No hail was required by PW under 34.2. She is only required to hail if she makes an alteration of course which was unforeseen. This clearly was not the case as both port gybe yachts were aware of yacht S. PL was disqualified.

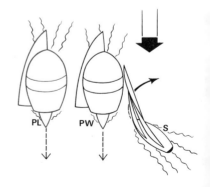

Rule 42.1(a)
IYRU Case 21. Overlaps on widely differing courses. L, on starboard tack, approached a starboard hand mark close-hauled. W approached from almost directly upwind and called for room to round the mark inside L. At all material times W had an overlap on L under the definition and was therefore entitled to room under Rule 42.1(a).

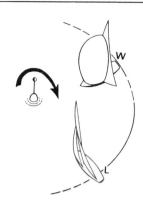

Rule 42.1(a)

IYRU Case 40. An interpretation of 'room'. 'Room' means, enough space to enable the inside boat, in the prevailing conditions and handled in a seamanlike manner, to pass in safety between the object and the outside boat.

Rule 42.1(a)

IYRU Case 50. When a mark is 'passed'. W and L were overlapped at a mark. L gave W adequate room. The Protest Committee found as a fact that W was unnecessarily slow in luffing up, and disqualified W after contact with L under 37.1. When adequate room at a mark has been given under 42.1(a) the basic rules apply again.

97
98
99

Rule 42.1(a)
IYRU Case 59. Tacking within the two lengths circle. Approaching a starboard hand windward mark, P passed close astern of S and tacked on to starboard completing it within two lengths of the mark. The two lengths determinative of Rule 42.3(a)(ii) does not therefore apply. P can claim room to round inside S provided she gains an overlap before the start of S's rounding manoeuvre. See also Case 59 under Rule 42.2(a).

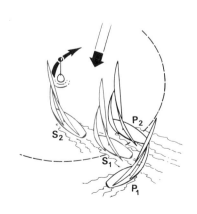

136

97 **98** **99** **97**	**Rule 42.1(a)**	*IYRU Case 76. Room at an obstruction. New overlap starts after tacking.* Two overlapping yachts were close-hauled. Both tacked and a new overlap began at that point which was more than two lengths from an obstruction. The new outside yacht was obliged to give the inside yacht room under Rule 42.1(a).
99 **77**	**Rule 42.1(e)**	*IYRU Case 62. After the mark—turning to a proper course.* An inside yacht without luffing rights, having been given room to round a mark, must assume her new proper course, under Rule 38.2, as soon as she is able to do so. If bearing away to a proper course includes a need to gybe, then she must gybe as required in 42.1(e). Proper course changes when the inside boat gets about half way past the mark. See also definition of Proper Course.
101	**Rule 42.2(a)**	*IYRU Case 68. Anticipation during rounding or passing marks or obstructions.* A line of yachts, each clear astern of the next ahead, are passing a continuous obstruction, the shore line. Even though a yacht ahead gybes on to port, a starboard tack yacht clear astern still has to keep clear in anticipation of the rounding or passing manoeuvre since Rule 42 applies. (Here the clause is 42.2(a).)

101

Rule 42.2(a)
IYRU Case 59. Overtaking when about to round a mark. When A came within two lengths of the mark, L had a leeward overlap on A; B had a windward overlap on L. L was therefore not an 'intervening yacht'. B was, however, overhauling A and L fast, but had no rights to room on A's windward side.
B is entitled to room between A and L under 42.1(a) but must keep clear of A under 42.2(a).

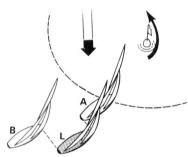

101

102

Rule 42.2(c)
IYRU Case 26. Yacht clear ahead—tacking round a mark. Approaching a windward mark close-hauled, A is clear ahead but to leeward of B. A cannot tack if she thereby infringes Rule 41. B, however, can hold her course to prevent A tacking. Rule 42.2(c) governs the situation.

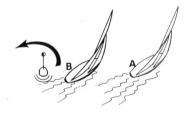

102

Rule 42.3
IYRU Case 71. Overlap limitations at marks. A group of yachts were reaching to a mark, gybing round it, and returning on a reciprocal course. A yacht which has to swing wide, or is carried by the current through the two lengths circle, and out beyond its limits, has to re-establish rounding rights under 42.3(a).

Rule 42.3(a)
IYRU Case 45. Opposite tacks—
overtaking. W and L were running on
port tack. S overtakes first L and
then W and intervenes between
them. S has right of way under Rule
36 over both port tack yachts, conse-
quently W does not rank as an
obstruction to S and Rule 42.3(a)
does not apply between S and L.

42.3(a) and (b)   *IYRU Case 67. Establishing an overlap at a continuous obstruction.* W and
L were running overlapped on the same gybe towards the finish, almost
two lengths apart. M overtook and intervened, establishing overlaps on
both yachts. There was no contact but W protested that M was not entitled
to room.

L and W were within two lengths of each other and so each yacht was
an obstruction with respect to the other two. L was a continuous obstruction to W and, under Rule 42.3(b) M established a legal overlap which
was shown by there being no contact thereafter.

42.3(b)   *IYRU Case 27. Rules for establishing overlaps on continuous obstructions—*
other yachts. See also Case 27 under Rule 37 which governs cases where
a yacht overhauls a line of yachts abreast and tries to intervene. The yachts
ahead form continuing obstructions and so the yacht clear astern may
not try to establish an overlap under Rule 43.3(b) unless there is room
to do so and to pass right through in safety (i.e. without touching either
yacht ahead).

42.3(b)   *IYRU Case 69. Establishing overlaps on continuous obstructions—the shore*
line. The rule is that no attempt to establish an overlap may be made
unless the yacht can do so and pass in safety. 'Safety' means—without
touching the yacht ahead or running aground.

When a successful overlap is established, the overtaking yacht can claim
room under Rule 42.1(a) and cannot be luffed into the obstruction.

42.3(c)   *IYRU Case 55. Luffing—definition of 'to windward of a mark'.* L employed
the well known tactic to try to shake off an overtaking boat on approaching a mark by luffing sharply, then bearing away to put W directly astern.
There was no hail. The question was—did she luff W 'to windward of
the mark' and if so did the manoeuvre come under Rule 42.3(c)

The definition is given as being the crossing of a line at right angles to
the direct course from the previous mark.

When 42.3(c) does apply the required hail must be specific. 'Luffing' is
not usually adequate. 'Luffing to windward of the mark' would be acceptable.

42.3(c)   *IYRU Case 60. Hailing when luffing.* A hail is not required when luffing
on open water, but only when she is 'about to round a mark' and is luffing
a boat to windward of it.

105	**Rule 42.3(c)**	*IYRU Case 61. Luffing to windward of a mark—the luffed yacht tacks* When a luffed yacht elects to break away by tacking before reaching the 'to windward of the mark' line, the luffing yacht is no longer obliged to pass 'to windward of the mark'.
107	**Rule 42.4**	*IYRU Case 54. Anti-barging rule complements Rule 37.* Rule 42.4 is a rule of exception to the basic rule in a special situation, but this does not mean that the basic rule is totally overridden or in abeyance. It is only when there is conflict that the rule of exception takes precedence. In the case of barging at the start the basic rule is usually complementary to Rule 42.4.
108	**Rule 43.2(a)**	*IYRU Case 6. Responding to a hail to tack at an obstruction.* W and L, close-hauled and overlapped on port tack, were approached by S, close-hauled on starboard tack. S hailed for water; L hailed W to avoid S but obtained no response to three hails. S bore away to avoid a collision with L. S protested L. W retired. The Appeals Committee ruled that L did enough to satisfy her obligations. She was entitled to expect W to respond. She was not obliged to bear away astern of S or to anticipate W's failure to comply with Rule 43.2(a).
	Rule 43	*IYRU Case 80. The amount of room required when tacking at an obstruction.* After a reply of 'You Tack' to L's hail on approaching an obstruction, L tacked and was able to avoid W, but she cannot claim that her 'loss of distance' in doing so entitles her to succeed in a protest against W.
	Rule 43	*IYRU Case 93. Close-hauled on opposite tacks near a continuing obstruction.* A close-hauled port tack yacht which is sailing close to, and parallel with, a continuing obstruction, must be prepared for a starboard tack yacht approaching on a collision course and to take early avoiding action. Rule 43 does not apply since they are on opposite tacks.
108 **109**	**Rule 43.1**	*IYRU Case 117.* Two yachts approaching the shore on starboard tack. The leeward yacht a length ahead and a length-and-a-half to leeward. The leeward yacht hails but is not heard. W does not respond but L tacks, tries to bear away underneath the stern of W but hits her several feet forward of the transom. On this occasion it seems that the hail was not adequate and a second louder hail should have been made. L was disqualified under Rule 36
112 **113** **114**	**Rule 44**	*IYRU Case 81. Rights of a premature starter.* W and L were overlapped at the start, sailing close-hauled. Both were premature starters though W was unaware of this fact. W's rights under Rule 42.2 were confined to those conferred by Rule 35 until the moment L bore away to return and re-start, at which moment she acquired full rights in respect of L not knowing she was a premature starter and not attempting to re-start. L, in bearing away to re-start was therefore required to keep clear of W under 44.1(a). In this case her tiller touched W and so she was disqualified.

Rule 45.1

IYRU Case 126. Yachts O and I rounded a mark to port, overlapped. Yacht O was rounding a second time, exonerating herself from having hit the mark, but giving yacht I room to round inside her. Both yachts bore away on starboard gybe to assume their proper courses to the next mark. I, the inside yacht, unexpectedly made a controlled gybe onto port causing the sails of the two yachts to touch. The protest committee disqualified O for failing to give sufficient room to I under Rule 45.1.

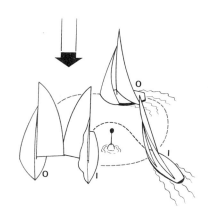

PART V—OTHER SAILING RULES

Rule 50

IYRU Case 34. Ranking as a starter. Shortly before the starting signal was made, the race was postponed, but this did not prevent several yachts starting and sailing the course. The new race was started but the other yachts did not return. They were recorded as not having started since they were not in the vicinity of the starting line.

Rule 50

IYRU Case 111. Ranking as a Starter. Several yachts were on the course side of the line at the starting gun. Some were half a mile away. The Race Officer did not fire a second gun as he was required to do to signify individual recalls, nor was the class flag flown at the 'dip'. The nearest yacht to the line, A, some 20 yards from the line, thought she was in the clear and sailed the race from which she was subsequently disqualified. However, she did rank as a starter under Rule 50 being in the vicinity of the line. And she was therefore subject to Rule 8.1 (Recalls) and 51.1(a) and (b) Sailing the course and should be granted some redress.

Rule 51.1(a)

IYRU Case 102. Finishing instructions. The finishing definition cannot be overruled by a Sailing Instruction. There is no provision for allowing dispensation for other methods of finishing.

115
116
117

Rule 51

IYRU Case 124. Limit marks on the finishing line. The inner limit mark was well on the post-finish side of the line. P crossed the line ahead of S, but well shorewards of the inner limit mark. Subsequently she passed the inner limit mark, leaving it to port. S, at the other end of the line, crossed the finishing line and left the outer limit mark to starboard. S

requested redress saying that the Race Officer had finished P before she
had rounded the inner limit mark and therefore before she had completed
the course.

The Protest Committee would not hear the protest and referred its decision for confirmation. This was forthcoming. A limit mark that lies on
the post-finish side of a finishing line does not rank as a mark.

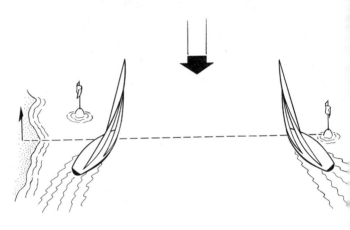

118
119

Rule 52.1

IYRU Case 41. Wrongfully compelled to touch a mark. When wrongfull
forced to touch a mark it is not enough to hoist a protest flag or expec
the other yacht to retire. A written protest must be lodged in order t
protect the case of the injured yacht so that the Race Committee coul
exonerate her under Rule 68.9.

Rule 52.1

IYRU Case 56. Wrongfully compelled to touch a mark—incorrect star
A yacht runs over a starting mark which sinks and re-surfaces, touchin
another yacht on its pre-start side. Thus the second yacht not only touche
the mark but failed to start correctly since she passed the mark on th
incorrect side. She has to return, re-start correctly or exonerate hersel
and protest the other yacht. Without the protest the Race Committee car
not consider redress under Rule 69.

Rule 52.1(b)
IYRU Case 120. Touching a mark.
Two yachts involved in a collision
and one of them hit the finishing
mark. This latter yacht neither protested nor exonerated herself by re-
rounding the mark and was disqualified. When a mark is touched the
yacht which makes the infringement
must either protest under Rule 68 or
exonerate herself by re-rounding.

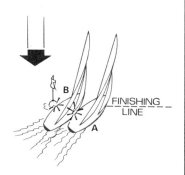

Rule 52.2

IYRU Case 64. Re-rounding marks. The effect of the rule is that a yacht
has to complete one rounding of the mark, in accordance with the requirements of the course, up to the point where she is on a proper course for
the next mark. Any fouling of the mark during this rounding is immaterial.
Thereafter she must make one complete penalty rounding without touching it.

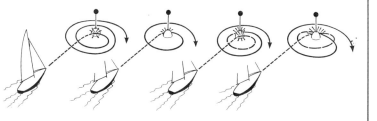

Rule 64.2
*IYRU Case 7. Definition of 'outrig-
ger'.* An outrigger is defined as a 'fitting'. The crew's hand is not a 'fitting' and can therefore be used to
hold a sheet outboard.

	Rule 60	*IYRU Case 66. Outside assistance etcetera.* A yacht lost a man overboard but took some time lowering spinnaker and preparing to recover him (Rule 57). Meanwhile a spectator boat picked up the man and returned him aboard the yacht. This did not contravene Rule 60 because of the specific exception to receiving outside assistance contained therein.
120	**Rule 54**	*IYRU Case 9. Dropping and hauling up an anchor.* To avoid infringing Rule 54, the anchor may not be thrown forward when being dropped. Furthermore, the action of hauling in the anchor line must not be so rapid that considerable way over the ground is generated at the point when the anchor leaves the bottom. No criterion is suggested but the Race Committee should decide on the evidence if advantage has been gained thereby.
	Rule 54.1(b)	*IYRU Case 92. Unfair propulsion—roll tacking.* Repeated roll tacking in calm or near calm conditions falls into the same category as 'pumping' and infringes Rule 54. It is the intention of the new Rule 54 to prevent a yacht coming out of a tack faster than it went into the tack.
	Rules 53, 55	*IYRU Case 94. Hauling out on an island also used as a turning mark.* Rules 53 and 55, when they apply, overrule the provisions of Rule 52.

PART VI—PROTESTS, DISQUALIFICATIONS AND APPEALS

121	**Rule 68.2**	*IYRU Case 47. Failure to display a protest flag.* A yacht which has knowledge of the facts of an incident, but is not certain of the rules, must nevertheless first show a protest flag, which can be withdrawn later if it appears that no infringement took place.
121	**Rule 68.4**	*IYRU Case 92. Informing a yacht protested against.* It is mandatory that a protesting yacht shall try to inform the yacht protested against that a protest will be lodged, but failure to succeed does not invalidate the protest. A claim by the protested yacht that she did not know she was being protested against is not a ground for not hearing the protest.
121	**Rule 68.4**	*IYRU Case 104. Informing a yacht protested against.* An attempt to inform is mandatory. There is no time limit. It is not mandatory to succeed. When Appendix 3 (720° turns) applies it is required that the yacht is informed by hail and by protest flag. The hail is the most important and should be immediate, otherwise the protested yacht is unable to take advantage of the opportunity to exonerate herself. When the Race Committee is satisfied that a yacht has failed to 'try to inform' the protest may not be heard, but a yacht cannot be disqualified for this reason.
121	**Rule 69**	*IYRU Case 88. Race Committees obligations.* Rule 69 permits relief when an act or omission of the Race Committee has resulted in prejudice to a competitor. In this case the complaint concerned Class Rules of which the Race Committee cannot be expected to have full knowledge. Rule 13 may only be invoked by the Committee at their discretion. It cannot be used by a competitor to accomplish what he had failed to do by means of a normal protest.
	Rule 69	*IYRU Case 75. Seeking redress from a Race Committee.* Action taken under Rule 69 does not require the display of a protest flag.

ule 69	*IYRU Case 74. Seeking redress from a Race Committee.* In a case where the sailing instructions for altering course were not correctly referred to as required under Rule 3.1 it was clear that a yacht's chances of winning were prejudiced. Accordingly a decision to abandon and re-sail under Rule 69 was appropriate.	**121**

ule 69   *IYRU Case 95. Seeking redress—criteria.* In this case the Race Committee found as a fact that no yachts were materially prejudiced, or that the race was unfair. A yacht may not protest against the Race Committee, but she may seek redress only if her finishing position has been prejudiced.

ule 70.2(b)   *IYRU Case 18. A late protest.* After a race it came to the notice of the Race Committee that a yacht had touched a starting line mark and neglected to take appropriate action. In spite of the fact that Declarations were not required, the terms of Rule 13 enable the Race Committee to take action under Rule 70.2(b).

ule 70.4   *IYRU Case 123. Measurer's Responsibility.* Two IOR rated yachts in a   **121** summer long series. One yacht, yacht A, was found to have sailed the series with an incorrect rating certificate. B requested redress under Rule 69. It was subsequently found by the national rating authority that there was an error in the rating certificate dating from the first hull measurement some years back. The protest committee found that the owner of yacht A was not responsible for the error and that he had not infringed Rule 19. The protest committee decided that the race committee was not responsible for the error and therefore yacht B was not entitled to redress under Rule 69. The protest could not be heard under Rule 70.4 because no measurer had been appointed for that series. Retrospective action for faulty rating certificates relating to yachts in a series would mean that no series could be concluded, which is simply not acceptable.

ule 71.1   *IYRU Case 48. No disqualification without a hearing.* In an incident between three yachts, one of them was not included in the hearing even though she was clearly involved, and it transpired that she was almost certainly at fault. She cannot be penalized. Also, in this case the facts had to be determined without her evidence.

ule 71.1   *IYRU Case 90. No disqualification without a hearing.* The Race Committee considered, incorrectly, that a yacht had not been entered in the manner prescribed, and therefore decided she was a non-starter, and was not awarded finishing points. She should not have been penalized without a hearing.

ule 74.1   *IYRU Case 77. Decisions based on facts.* In a protest resulting from contact between boats, a Race Committee must find the relevant facts and make a decision based on them.
If there was no contact and the evidence is insufficient or conflicting the Race Committee may dismiss the protest on the grounds that it is not satisfied that there was an infringement of the rules.

ule 75.2   *IYRU Case 78. Protest for bad manners or sportsmanship.* A Race Committe may exclude a yacht from a series, including races already completed, for a gross infringement of good manners or sportsmanship. In this case it would not be enough to disqualify the yacht from the race concerned in the protest since she would have still succeeded in her aim and have won the series.

| **Rule 77** | *IYRU Case 119. Right of appeal.* A yacht protested the Race Committee because of inadequate rescue facilities in contravention of the clubs deed. The Race Committee cancelled the completed race. A second yacht appealed the decision. However the second yacht had no right to appeal as she was not a party to the hearing of the request for redress by the first yacht. She herself must request redress. |

APPENDICES TO THE RULES

| **Appendix 3** | *IYRU Case 100. 720° turns penalty.* It is mandatory for the protesting yacht to hail effectively immediately, otherwise the infringing yacht is prevented from taking advantage of the alternative penalty. The hoisting of a protest flag is also required but can follow the hail. |
| **Appendix 6** | *IYRU Case 104. Procedure when yacht is not informed of a protest.* A yacht must 'try to inform' at the first reasonable opportunity which is normally immediately, and, in the case of 720° turns penalties, is essentially immediately by hail if the offending yacht is to have an opportunity to take advantage of this. When the Race Committee is satisfied that a protest flag was flown at the earliest reasonable opportunity, failure to inform by hail is not grounds for refusing to hear the protest. When a yacht fails to try to inform, the protest may not be heard but the protesting yacht may not be disqualified for this reason. |